SEA SNAKES

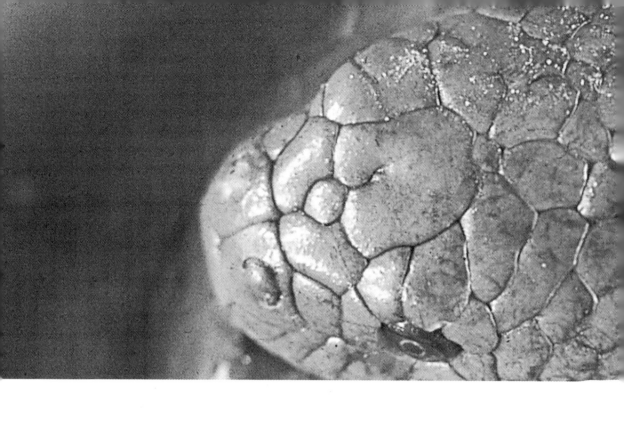

SEA SNAKES

Harold Heatwole

 Krieger Publishing Company
Malabar, Florida

This book is dedicated to my research assistants and technicians, past and present, a hard-working and reliable core of people upon whom so much of my scientific endeavour has depended. Many of them subsequently embarked on their own research careers. They have contributed far more than is reflected in their meagre salaries (indeed many were unpaid volunteers). They have my lasting gratitude for their friendship, diligence and professionalism.

Adrian Wenner	Elizabeth Davison	Petah Abbott
Don Davis	Sue Murdaugh	Menna Jones
Frank Torres	Sue Harrington	Peter King
Faustino MacKenzie	Judy Herrington	Becky Francis
Sheila Blasini	Dominique Rowell	Louise Percival
Isabel Colorado	Robert Muir	Sandra Hamdorff
Sara Armstrong	Amor Ferjiani	Zoltan Enoch
Abel Rossy	Sue Wilson	David Dye
John Veron	Jacqueline Wilson	Keith Cornish
Audry Yoder Heatwole	Lynda Bridges	Judy Powell
Elizabeth Cameron	Sheryl Greathead	Bryan Stuart
Terrence Done	Maria McCoy	Naseem Ostavar

The book is also dedicated to the myriad students and friends who pitched in and helped out on particular short-term projects and expeditions.

Original Edition 1987
University of New South Wales Press

Second Edition 1999
University of New South Wales Press Ltd
and

Krieger Publishing Company
Exclusive distributor for: Americas (North, Central, & South), Caribbean, Europe, and Africa.
1725 Krieger Drive
Malabar, FL 32950-3323 USA
Tel: (407) 724-9542 Fax: (407) 951-3671
info@krieger-pub.com

Library of Congress Cataloguing-In-Publication Data:
A catalog record for this book is available from the Library of Congress, Washington, DC.

ISBN 1-57524-116-1

10 9 8 7 6 5 4 3 2

Printer Everbest Printing, Hong Kong

CONTENTS

PREFACE

Part of the reason I became an Australian had to do with sea snakes. The unique nature of the Australian fauna had always fascinated me. After the famous and charismatic kangaroos, wombats, koalas and platypuses already covered in this series, the Australian snakes came high on my list of interests, particularly the sea snakes which were only beginning to be studied ecologically and physiologically at the time I immigrated to Australia.

Thus it was that in 1966 while sitting in my office at the University of Puerto Rico examining an invitation to apply for a position at the University of New England in New South Wales, I considered the proposition a full 20 seconds before reaching for my pen to write a positive response. This was the beginning of an involvement with both Australia and sea snakes that has persisted. I became an Australian citizen and I am still studying sea snakes, although the latter has carried me far from the shores of Australia, throughout the range of sea snakes, and has involved me in collaboration with colleagues from Japan, the United States and France, as well as with fellow Australians.

Soon after my arrival in Australia, I contacted the Deputy Hydrographer of the Royal Australian Navy, J.H.S. Osborn, with a request for assistance in getting to parts of the Great Barrier Reef where sea snakes were abundant. Presently I found myself as a guest aboard a minesweeper, HMAS *Teal*, on a month-long sovereignty cruise of the reef. That was followed by a month as a participant in the Belgian Expedition to the Great Barrier Reef aboard the Belgian corvette, *DeMoor*. At intervals thereafter I undertook various trips with the Queensland Lighthouse Service on maintenance and supply vessels. I went on an expedition with *National Geographic* magazine and on various research trips with the Australian National Parks and Wildlife Service. Further opportunities to conduct field work arose through my participation in the production of television documentaries on sea snakes by Ron and Valerie Taylor, Ben and Eva Cropp, Grundy Productions, and Wild Kingdom. Eventually I organised my own expeditions through grants from the Australian Research Grants Committee and from Marine and Sciences Technology. I was invited to participate in two international expeditions aboard the *Alpha Helix*, a floating physiology laboratory from Scripps Oceanographic Institution, and later participated in the Acheron Expedition emanating from New Zealand.

In the course of these expeditions, I forged long-term friendships and professional links with outstanding scientists and naturalists who shared the curiosity, excitement, fascination and sometimes danger of making direct acquaintance with these marvellous animals. I am grateful to these colleagues who have enriched my intellectual and personal life so much. Especially noteworthy among them are Harold Cogger, Sherman Minton, Bill Dunson, Nobuo Tamiya, Toru Tamiya, Roger Seymour, André Ménez, Harvey Lillywhite and those of my PhD students whose dissertations dealt with sea snakes: Ken Zimmerman, Shantay Zimmerman and Glen Burns. All will recognise their own contributions to sea snake research in the following pages. This book gives an account of what has been learned about sea snakes and, in so doing, indicates what remains unknown and has yet to be discovered by those that follow.

This book is based on an earlier one entitled *Sea Snakes* published in 1987 by the University of New South Wales Press. The previous book has been out of print for a number of years. During the intervening time a number of advances have been made in the study of sea snakes and much new information has accumulated. The present book brings this material up to date and provides a greater photographic coverage. However, progress has been uneven in different aspects of sea snake biology. Some fields have moved ahead significantly, whereas in others little new information has been obtained since the previous book was published. Accordingly, some chapters have been lengthened or expanded into several new chapters. Other chapters have not changed much, new information being merely woven into the fabric of the existing matrix. The manuscript benefited greatly from the constructive criticism of Harold Voris, Hal Cogger and Mike Guinea, from the expertise of Chris Smith in computers and electronic transmission, and from the editorial pen of Louise Egerton.

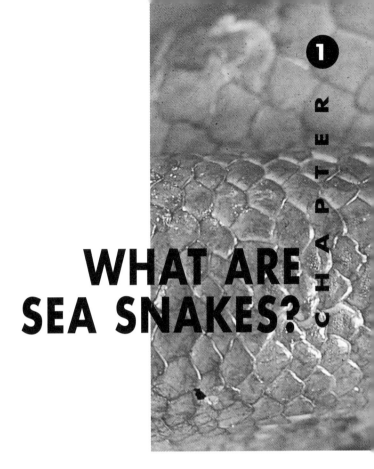

WHAT ARE SEA SNAKES?

Sea snakes are real, air-breathing snakes with body scales, forked tongues, lidless eyes, no legs and all of the other attributes one associates with land snakes. They are not peculiar kinds of eels as many people believe. Eels are fish with gills; sea snakes are true reptiles with lungs.

Sea snakes do differ subtly from land snakes in physiology and body structure in ways that will be described later. However, the similarities of these two groups of snakes are more conspicuous than are their differences and their close relationship is obvious, even at a glance.

Unlike some of the animals treated in this series, such as the platypus and the wombat, sea snakes are not unique to Australia. As a group, they are widely distributed in the Indian and Pacific oceanic regions, and even some individual species have extensive geographic ranges. This book garners information about marine snakes from all parts of their geographic range.

THE KINDS OF SEA SNAKES

Sea snakes are not a single biological entity. Rather, they are comprised of snakes of several different kinds that separately have become adapted to living in the sea. Accordingly, various families of snakes contain marine representatives that collectively are designated as sea snakes. Of the 15 living families of snakes, four contain marine species (Figure 1.1, Table 1.1, Appendix 1). They are the families Colubridae (colubrid snakes), Acrochordidae (file snakes or elephant-trunk snakes), Laticaudidae (sea kraits) and Hydrophiidae (true sea snakes).

The largest family of snakes is the Colubridae with about 290 genera and 1500 species, most of which are terrestrial or arboreal. This family contains the majority of non-venomous snakes of the world as well as some species that are venomous or mildly venomous. Two of its 14 sub-

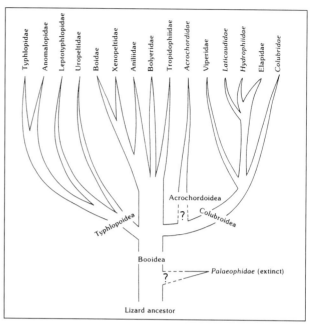

families, the Homalopsinae and the Natricinae, tend strongly toward an aquatic lifestyle. There are 11 genera and about 35 species of homalopsines. All are aquatic and nine species inhabit salty water (Plates 1–4). The subfamily Natricinae contains 37 genera and about 185 species. Although they are known as 'water snakes', many are only semi-aquatic and some are terrestrial, burrowing or arboreal. Only a few species and races of one genus, *Nerodia* (Plate 5) occur in salty water. *Nerodia* is non-venomous.

The family Acrochordidae contains only one genus with three species, two of which are found only in freshwater. The third, the granulated file snake (*Acrochordus granulatus*) (Plate 6), occurs in a variety of aquatic habitats ranging from freshwater streams and ponds to estuaries, mangrove swamps and the sea. It is characterised by a loose, granular skin. File snakes seldom, if ever, leave the water. File snakes are non-venomous.

The venomous sea snakes are treated here as two families, the Laticaudidae and the Hydrophiidae. These two families are closely related to each other and to the terrestrial cobras (family Elapidae).

The family Laticaudidae contains only one genus (*Laticauda*) (Plate 7) with four species, all of which are marine except for *Laticauda crockeri* that lives in Lake Te-Nggano on Rennell Island, Solomon Islands. The Hydrophiidae (Plates 8–14) contains 16 genera and 54 species, all but one of which are marine. The sole exception is *Hydrophis semperi* that inhabits the fresh water of Lake Taal in the Philippines.

Figure 1.1
Phylogenetic tree of the superfamilies and families of snakes. Extinct terrestrial families of the superfamilies *Booidea* and Colubroidea are not shown. Italicised families have at least some species inhabiting salt water.

Table 1.1

Marine and estuarine snakes

Family & Genus	No. in the family	No. of species
Family HYDROPHIIDAE (TRUE SEA SNAKES)	53	
Acalyptophis		1
Aipysurus		8
Astrotia		1
Disteira		4
Emydocephalus		2
Enhydrina		1
Ephalophis		1
Hydrelaps		1
Hydrophis		27*
Kerilia		1
Kolpophis		1
Lapemis		1
Parahydrophis		1
Pelamis		1
Thalassophina		1
Thalassophis		1
Family LATICAUDIDAE (SEA KRAITS)	4*	
Laticauda		4*
Family COLUBRIDAE (COLUBRIDS)		
Subfamily HOMALOPSINAE** (HOMALOPSINES)	9	
Bitia		1
Cantoria		2
Cerberus		1
Enhydris		2
Fordonia		1
Gerarda		1
Myron		1
Subfamily NATRICINAE (NATRICINES)	3	
*Nerodia***		3
Family ACROCHORDIDAE (FILE SNAKES)	1	
*Acrochordus***		1
TOTAL 70		

* Excluding one freshwater species.
**Additional freshwater species may occasionally enter salty water.

Of the 70 species of marine snakes known, 53 (76 per cent) are hydrophiids, nine (13 per cent) are homalopsines, four (6 per cent) are laticaudids, three (4 per cent) are natricines and one species (1 per cent) is an acrochordid.

Taxonomists do not agree completely on the status of some taxa. For example, some would break up the large genus of *Hydrophis* into several genera and opinions differ as to whether particular populations belong to the same or different species. As much as possible, I have adjusted nomenclature in this book to conform to the most commonly accepted classification but the data at hand were not always sufficient to allow this to be done with confidence for all regions. For the laticaudids and hydrophiids, I have followed the nomenclature published in a checklist by P. Golay and his colleagues in 1993. The nomenclature for the homalopsines follows a revision of that sub-family by Ko Ko Gyi in 1970, and that for the natricines follows the handbook by Albert and Anna Wright in 1957.

ORIGIN AND EVOLUTION OF SEA SNAKES

Snakes comprise the most recently evolved group of reptiles. They clearly originated from lizards and share many features with them. It was long thought that snakes probably originated from legless burrowing lizards but more recent evidence points toward a marine ancestor. Snakes probably first arose in the late Jurassic (somewhat more than 135 million years ago) because the first known fossils are from the next geological period, the Cretaceous. The most primitive of these fossil snakes, *Pachyrhachis problematicus*, had a well-developed sacrum, pelvis and hindlimbs and is the only known snake with functional limbs. It was marine and was related to the mosasaurs, a group of Cretaceous marine lizards.

Other snakes from the Cretaceous are known only from incomplete fossils and as no good skull material exists the most that can be said of them is that they were snakes with some characteristics intermediate between those of lizards and modern snakes. The family to which they belong, the Paleophidae, persisted as late as the Eocene, about 50 million years ago, before becoming extinct. At least three genera of paleophids — *Anomalopsis*, *Palaeophis* and *Ptenosphenus* — appear to have been marine, and some palaeophid remains are associated with those of primitive whales. This ancient group of snakes was widespread and is known from the Tertiary deposits of Europe, North America, South America and Africa.

The paleophids were an evolutionary side-branch that became extinct without giving rise to any later forms. Thus, modern sea snakes evolved a marine lifestyle secondarily from ancestors that already had become terrestrial, and present-day marine adaptations are rather recent developments. Except for the Acrochordidae of unknown age, the families of snakes with marine members are geologically quite young. The colubrids did not appear until the Oligocene, less than 40 million years ago, and the elapids, which developed from the colubrids, are first known from the Miocene, less than 30 million years ago. Both the laticaudids and the hydrophiids arose from the elapids, and although there are no known fossils of these two families, they must be younger than their elapid ancestors.

Marine tendencies arose independently within several separate terrestrial lineages: once in the line leading to the homalopsines, once in the file snakes, probably at least twice in the ancestry of the venomous sea snakes (separately in the laticaudids and hydrophiids), and finally, incipiently in the natricines (Figure 1.1).

The phylogenetic relationships of the file snakes are not clear. Herpetologists have differing opinions. Some believe them to be colubrids and would place them in the subfamily Natricinae of that family. Others consider them in a separate family, Acrochordidae, but closely related to the colubrids. Still others think they are related to pythons. More recently, however, an assessment of the morphology of these snakes, as well as an analysis of their antigenic responses to the plasma proteins of snakes of other families, have indicated that they have no close affinities with any other living group of snakes. They are now placed in their own superfamily Acrochordoidea (Figure 1.1). Until the fossil record becomes more completely known, some doubt will probably remain about the precise ancestry of file snakes.

In file snakes the marine habit clearly has developed independently. Two of the species inhabit fresh water whereas the third lives in both fresh and salty water. Either this family was originally marine with two of the species later radiating into fresh water exclusively, or they were originally from fresh water with *Acrochordus granulatus* subsequently becoming partly marine.

None of the saltwater races of *Nerodia* are completely separate from freshwater populations. Although these races are morphologically, behaviourally and perhaps physiologically distinct, they seem to interbreed with freshwater races. It would appear that these natricines represent early stages in the evolution of adaptation to salt water and are only beginning to acquire marine tendencies.

The phylogenetic relationships of venomous sea snakes are still confused and a number of conflicting ideas are current. One idea is that all species had a common origin within the Elapidae (cobra family). It was believed that there was an early divergence, one line leading to the sea kraits and the other to the remaining venomous sea snakes (true sea snakes). The former were placed in the subfamily Laticaudinae and the latter in the subfamily Hydrophiinae; to show their supposed common origin, both subfamilies were grouped in one family, Hydrophiidae. More recent biochemical evidence has led some herpetologists to feel that sea kraits are so closely related to the other venomous sea snakes that they should not be placed in a separate subfamily but merely a separate genus (*Laticauda*) within the family Hydrophiidae. Still other authors do not completely accept that sea kraits and true sea snakes had a common marine ancestor, rather they believe that they developed independently from different stocks of terrestrial elapids: the sea kraits from southeastern Asian elapids and the true sea snakes from Australian elapids. This view is reflected in the allocation of sea kraits to their own family, Laticaudidae, and all of the true sea snakes to a separate one, Hydrophiidae, or alternatively grouping the Australian terrestrial elapids with the true sea snakes into the Hydrophiidae. Still other herpetologists consider the relationship between sea kraits, true sea snakes and terrestrial elapids so close that all are lumped together into the Elapidae.

These different ideas are merely variations on a theme or nuances of interpretation. Regardless of which classification scheme one chooses, it is clear that the sea snakes and sea kraits are only slightly modified cobras (elapids). It will be some time before the precise relations of sea kraits and true sea snakes are understood completely. Whether or not they shared a common marine ancestor and regardless of the number of stocks of terrestrial elapids that might have been involved, keeping these two groups in separate families emphasises some of the distinctive features of their biology and is the approach adopted in this book.

GIANT 'SEA SERPENTS'

The sea serpents of mythology were reported to be awesome beasts of enormous size. They were credited with such exploits as coiling around ships and seizing men from the decks (Figure 1.2). Like the Loch Ness monster, 'sea serpents' have been reported at frequent intervals over a long period and, although there is some weak circumstantial evidence in support of their existence, no indisputable proof has yet been offered. There are no unequivocal photographs, and purported specimens invariably have turned out to be partly decayed basking sharks or other well-known large marine animals. Nevertheless, the notion that large 'sea serpents' or sea monsters exist does not die easily. People believing in their reality point out that:

1. some large marine animals that were long considered mythical, such as the kraken or giant squid, later became documented by specimens
2. some whales are known only from a few stranded bodies or a few skulls, with no living individuals having ever been seen
3. most reported sightings of 'sea serpents' since the advent of noisy, engine-powered ships have occurred where disturbance is minimal outside of the major shipping channels.

They interpret these facts to mean that even very large sea creatures may escape notice indefinitely and not be captured by the camera lens or reach the museum curator's table if they are shy enough to avoid commercial shipping lanes.

Figure 1.2
Two fourteenth-century Venetian woodcuts illustrating the common misconception of sea snakes at that time.
(From Heuvelmens 1968)

Many reports of 'sea serpents' were obvious hoaxes or the product on an overwrought imagination. However, after spurious and fanciful accounts are weeded out, there remains a body of information provided by serious, sober people not given to sensationalism or exaggeration that cannot be ignored. Even such a reputable scientific organisation as Scripps Institution of Oceanography prepared and put into operation traps to capture sea monsters just in case such animals did exist.

Bernard Heuvelmans, a Belgian zoologist, examined in minute detail all of the available information embodied in the reported sightings from antiquity up to the date of his study (1965). He sieved out the hoaxes and illusions as best he could and fed the remaining data into a computer. The results were surprising. The characteristics of the sea monsters fell neatly into nine categories, each of which was consistent over a number of independent reports over several centuries; in most cases the persons reporting the sightings probably were unaware of any previous reports. Dr Heuvelmens interpreted these categories as distinct species and went so far as to describe each one and give some of them scientific names. Should any of these really exist and be captured, they would have the novel status of having been properly described and named before officially being discovered!

The most amazing result from Heuvelmans' study was that particular descriptions were geographically consistent. Certain types of animals were reported only from particular regions and seemed to have definite geographic ranges. For example, sightings of what Dr Heuvelmans called the 'super-otter' occurred only in the Arctic Ocean, and those of the many-humped 'sea serpent' only in the North Atlantic; others had wider distributions such as the subtropical and tropical waters of the world. One he believed to be migratory on the basis of consistent sightings in one region only during a particular season and in a different area only at another season.

Although historically the terms 'sea monster' and 'sea serpent' were used interchangeably, the descriptions do not have a reptilian flavour, and Heuvelmans considered only one of his categories as possibly reptilian. That one was not a serpent (it resembled a large crocodile with flipper-like limbs). Five he believed to be mammals, some he thought might be large eel-like fish and others he could not allocate to any known animal group.

It is probably wise to maintain a healthy scepticism about the existence of 'sea serpents' and to regard them as mythical until better evidence is brought forward. Even if they do exist, the appellation is probably a misnomer as they almost certainly are not serpents or reptiles of any kind.

The real sea snakes, although diminutive in comparison to their mythical namesakes, hold their own aura of mystery. They are equally fascinating and much more amenable to investigation.

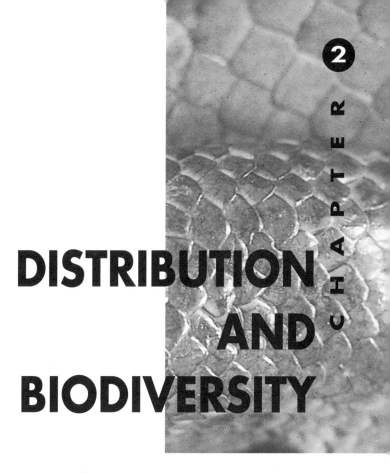

DISTRIBUTION AND BIODIVERSITY

With the exception of a few colubrid snakes in the subfamily Natricinae, all marine snakes are from the tropics or subtropics (Figures 2.1, 2.2). Their greatest diversity is in the waters of northern Australia, Malaysia and the Indonesian archipelago, with 24 species known from the Straits of Malacca alone. Thirty-seven species have been recorded from Australia and 36 from Indonesia/Malaysia.

As one proceeds peripherally from this region into the Indian and Pacific Oceans, the number of species generally decreases (Figure 2.3). For example, going northward from Australia there are 32 species in New Guinea, at least 16 in Cambodia/Vietnam, 15 in the Philippines, 19 from mainland China, 7–10 in Taiwan and eight (possibly nine) in Japan. Eastward, the Solomon Islands have seven, New Caledonia has eight, Vanuatu has at least six species, Fiji has at least four, Tonga has three, and Niue has two. Northwestward there are 30 species in Thailand, 18 from Burma (Myanmar), at least 12 from Bangladesh, 23 from India, 15–18 from Sri Lanka, 12 from Pakistan and ten from the Arabian Gulf. Beyond these limits, there is only one species, *Pelamis platurus*.

It is not always easy to identify the true geographic range of breeding populations of sea snakes merely from records of preserved

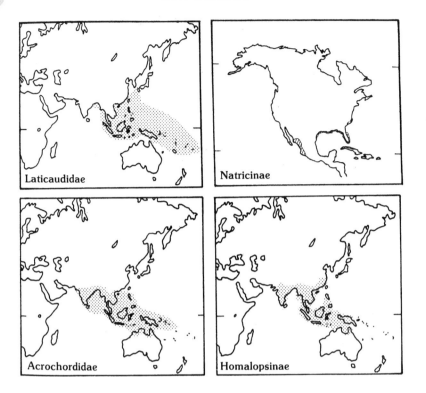

Figure 2.1 Geographic distribution of marine snakes in the families Laticaudidae and Acrochordidae, and the colubrid sub-families Natricinae and Homalopsinae.

specimens. Individuals often are swept well out of the range in which they breed when caught up in currents. Examples are the northern-most records of sea snakes from Korea and southwestern Siberia (about latitude 45°N) and individuals of *Pelamis platurus* and *Laticauda* species washed up on the shores of Tasmania and northern New Zealand, well outside of their normal breeding ranges. Perhaps these are accidentally transported by currents.

The hydrophiids or true sea snakes are the most widely distributed group of marine snakes. The yellow-bellied sea snake, (*Pelamis platurus*) (Plate 14) has the widest distribution of all, extending from the continental shelf of eastern Africa, along the coast of southern Asia and through the Australasian archipelago northward to Japan, south-ward along the eastern Australian coast and eastward across the Pacific Ocean, reaching waters of the western coast of the Americas (Figure 2.2). It is not usually found in the deeper waters but mostly in the shal-lower ones over continental shelves or around archipelagoes. Consequently, its distribution across the Pacific is discontinuous, with extensive gaps. Stray individuals occur as far south as Tasmania and New Zealand.

The other hydrophiids have more restricted distributions, not only

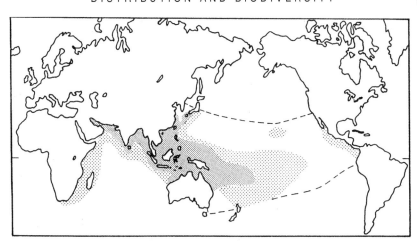

Figure 2.2
Distribution of snakes of the family Hydrophiidae. Fine stippling represents the collective range of all members of the family other than *Pelamis platurus*. Coarse stippling indicates the additional area occupied by *P. platurus*. Dotted lines enclose the area in which *P. platurus* sometimes occurs as strays carried by currents or storms.

as individual species but as a group. Their collective range extends along coastal waters from the Persian Gulf eastward into the tropical waters of Asia and Australia through the islands of the southwestern Pacific and northward to Japan and northeastern China (Figure 2.2).

The laticaudids or sea kraits are found in the waters of continental southeastern Asia, Indonesia, the Philippines, New Guinea and the southwestern Pacific islands (Figure 2.1).

Most colubrids are terrestrial or occupy fresh water. However, there are a few species of the subfamily Natricinae that inhabit saltmarshes and estuaries in temperate to subtropical North America (Figure. 2.1). These are *Nerodia fasciata clarki* from the saltmarshes of the Gulf of Mexico and southern Atlantic coasts of the United States, *Nerodia fasciata compressicauda* from the mangroves of Cuba and southern Florida, *Nerodia fasciata taeniata* from the saltmarshes of eastern Florida, *Nerodia sipedon williamengelsi* from the saltmarshes in North Carolina (Plate 5) and perhaps populations of *Nerodia valida* from the Pacific coast of Mexico. None of these colubrid natricines occupy deep water and none venture far from land. Some merely enter the water to feed.

The colubrid subfamily Homalopsinae occurs in India, southeastern Asia, Indonesia, the Philippines, Papua New Guinea, the Solomon Islands and northern Australia (Figure 2.1, Appendix 1). *Bitia hydroides* (Plate 1) from the coastal areas of Burma, Thailand and Malaysia, *Cantoria violacea* from the coasts of Burma and Malaysia and *Cantoria annulata* from New Guinea are thoroughly marine. Several species occupy mangrove swamps, estuaries and the lower reaches of rivers. These are the dog-faced snake or bockadam (*Cerberus rynchops*) (Plate 2), the white-bellied mangrove snake (*Fordonia leucobalia*) (Plate 3), and the mangrove snake (*Myron*

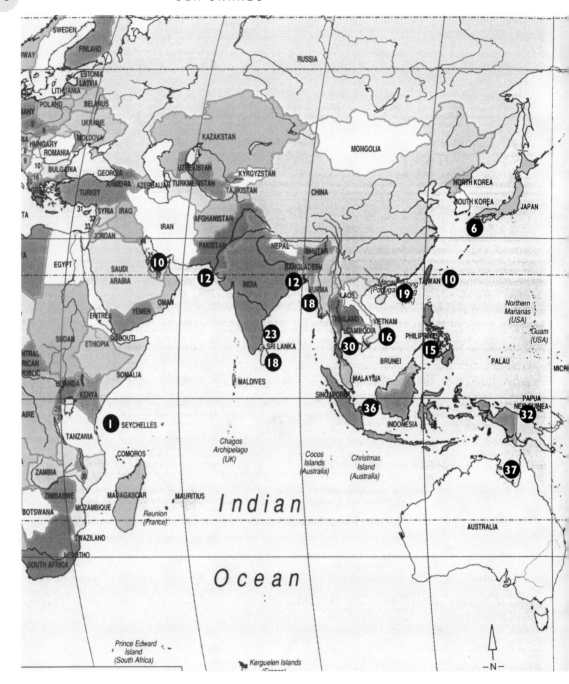

Figure 2.3
Map showing the number of species of marine snakes recorded for different
regions of the world. Note that the numbers of species progressively decrease
with increasing distance from Australasia.

Number of species per region: Arabian gulf 10 Bangladesh 12 Burma (Myanmar) 18 Fiji 4 French
Polynesia 1 India 23 Indonesia 36   China 19 Japan 8 Malaysia 36 Mexico 1 New Caledonia 8
Niue 2 Pakistan 12 Panama 1 Papua New Guinea 32 Philippines 15 Seychelles 1 Solomon Islands 7
Sri Lanka 18 Taiwan 10 Thailand 30 Tonga 2 USA 1 Vanuatu 6 Vietnam/Cambodia 16

richardsonii) (Plate 4). *Cerberus* and *Fordonia* are distributed in south-eastern Asia, the East Indian archipelago and northern Australia whereas *Myron* is confined to New Guinea and Australia. Another species, *Gerarda prevostiana*, occurs from India to Thailand and at least in the latter place inhabits mangroves. Finally, in the large and mainly freshwater genus *Enhydris*, two Chinese species, *Enhydris bennetti* and *Enhydris chinensis*, have been reported to enter the sea.

The acrochordids or file snakes have a similar distribution to the homalopsines (Figure 2.1, Appendix 1).

REGIONAL DISTRIBUTIONS

Many sea snakes are relatively rare and so may be overlooked unless collecting has been both intensive and extensive. For this reason, a particular species may not have been recorded from a country even though that country lies well within the general region known to be inhabited by that species. The following accounts of species of marine snakes from various countries are based on available regional studies that differ in completeness, reliability and date of publication. For this reason, they should be interpreted as indicating the minimal number of species present in a particular country; further investigation may expand the list.

Sea snakes recognise ecological boundaries, not political ones, and listing species by country is an artificial approach to biogeography. However, most faunal studies have been orientated around particular nations; accordingly, the information is presented in that way in the present chapter.

THE ARABIAN GULF

The family Hydrophiidae is the only group of marine snakes occurring in the Arabian Gulf and, except for *Pelamis platurus* that reaches the eastern coast of Africa, the Gulf marks the westernmost limit of that family.

J.N.B. Brown in collaboration with the Natural History Group of Dubai summarised the known sea snake fauna of the Gulf. After accounting for subsequent new records and taxonomic changes, there are five species of *Hydrophis* as well as five other genera (*Enhydrina*, *Lapemis*, *Thalassophina*, *Astrotia* and *Pelamis*), each with a single species, giving a total marine snake fauna of ten species.

PAKISTAN

Sherman Minton recorded 12 species from six genera of hydrophiids from Pakistan. After accounting for subsequent name changes, there were seven species of *Hydrophis* with the other five genera

(*Enhydrina*, *Thalassophina*, *Astrotia*, *Lapemis* and *Pelamis*) represented by only one species each.

There were reports of *Acrochordus granulatus* (family Acrochordidae) and the homalopsine *Cerberus rynchops* from the nineteenth century but no recent records. None of the other homalopsines from Pakistan are marine.

INDIA

T.S.N. Murthy reviewed the snakes of India and included 23 marine species of which one was an acrochordid (*Acrochodus granulatus*), two were laticaudids (*Laticauda colubrina* and *L. laticaudata*), 18 were hydrophiids and two were homalopsines (*Cerberus rynchops* and *Gerarda prevostiana*); the remaining Indian homalopsines occupy fresh water. Adjusting for more recent taxonomy, the hydrophiids included seven genera (*Kerilia*, *Thalassophina*, *Enhydrina*, *Hydrophis*, *Lapemis*, *Astrotia* and *Pelamis*) all represented by one species each except for *Hydrophis* that had 12.

SRI LANKA

Anslem de Silva reported the definite occurrence of 13 species of hydrophiids for Sri Lanka, of which seven were in the genus *Hydrophis* and one each in the genera *Astrotia*, *Enhydrina*, *Kerilia*, *Lapemis*, *Thalassophina* and *Pelamis* (after accounting for recent taxonomic and nomenclatural changes). He considered that two other species of *Hydrophis* and *Disteira nigrocincta* were likely to occur in the area also. The only marine homalopsine known to occur in Sri Lanka is *Gerarda prevostiana*. *Acrochordus granulatus* (family Acrochordidae) is also present, bringing the total known species of marine snakes to 15 and the probable number to 18.

BANGLADESH

Various manuals on venomous snakes were prepared by the military forces of the United States. These highlighted the most dangerous species and probably are incomplete. The hydrophiids listed for Bangladesh included five species of *Hydrophis* and one each of *Enhydrina*, *Lapemis* and *Thalassophina*. Two species of *Laticauda* (*L. colubrina* and *L. laticaudata*) also occur there, as does the homalopsine *Cerberus rynchops* and the acrochordid *Acrochordus granulatus*, making a total of at least 12 marine species.

BURMA (MYANMAR)

A military manual summarising the venomous marine snakes of Burma included four species of *Hydrophis* and one each of *Enhydrina*, *Kerilia*, *Lapemis*, *Aipysurus*, *Astrotia*, *Pelamis* and *Thalassophina*. Two species of *Laticauda*, the marine homalopsines *Bitia hydroides*, *Cerberus rynchops*, *Cantoria violacea* and *Gerarda provostiana* and the acrochordid *Acrochordus granulatus* also occur in Burma. This gives a total of 18 marine species.

THAILAND

John Murphy, Merel Cox and Harold Voris summarised the records of sea snakes from the Gulf of Thailand over the last 75 years and compiled an up-to-date list of the venomous species from that country. There were 24 species of hydrophiids of which 14 were of the genus *Hydrophis*; other genera were represented by only one species each and included *Aipysurus*, *Acalyptophis*, *Astrotia*, *Enhydrina*, *Kolpophis*, *Lapemis*, *Pelamis*, *Thalassophina* and *Thalassophis*. They discounted the presence of laticaudids in the Gulf. However, two laticaudids (*Laticauda colubrina* and *L. laticaudata*) are known from elsewhere in the country. In addition, the acrochordid *Acrochordus granulatus* and three of the Thai homalopsines occur in salt water (*Bitia hydroides*, *Cerberus rynchops* and *Cantoria violacea*), giving a total of 30 marine species.

CAMBODIA AND VIETNAM

Military manuals listed 11 species of hydrophiids from nine genera (*Aipysurus*, *Astrotia*, *Hydrophis*, *Kerilia*, *Lapemis*, *Pelamis*, *Thalassophina* and *Thalassophis*) after correcting for more recent taxonomy. Only four species of *Hydrophis* were included, almost certainly an underestimate.

Two laticaudids (*Laticauda colubrina* and *L. laticaudata*) also are present in the area. In addition, there are three species of marine homalopsines: *Cerberus rynchops*, *Fordonia leucobalia* and *Enhydris chinensis*. Thus, the total number of marine snakes is at least 16.

MALAYSIA AND INDONESIA

Indonesia and Malaysia have a combined marine snake fauna of 36 species, including 27 species of hydrophiids in ten genera (*Aipysurus*, *Astrotia*, *Disteira*, *Hydrophis*, *Kerilia*, *Enhydrina*, *Lapemis*, *Pelamis*, *Thalassophina* and *Thalassophis*), five species of homalopsines, three laticaudids and one *Acrochordus*.

AUSTRALIA

Australia has a rich marine snake fauna, with 32 species of hydrophiids, two species of laticaudids, one marine acrochordid and three marine or brackish species of homalopsines, giving a total of 38 species (Table 2.1). These encompass over half (59 per cent) of the world's species of marine snakes. All but four of the 16 known genera of hydrophiids have representatives in Australia, the absent ones being *Kerilia*, *Kolpophis*, *Thalassophina* and *Thalassophis*. The only species of marine acrochordid is distributed widely along the northern part of the country. In contrast, the homalopsines are not so well represented, only half of the six genera being present in Australia. Missing are *Bitia,* *Cantoria* and *Gerarda*. The sole genus of sea krait, *Laticauda*, occurs as breeding populations in New Guinea just across the narrow Torres Strait from Australia. However, there has been no verification of resident breeding populations of laticaudids in Australian waters and all records from continental Australia and Tasmania seem to be based on vagrant individuals.

The only taxonomic category of marine snakes above generic level that is not represented at all in Australia is the subfamily Natricinae.

Hydrophis is the largest genus of marine snakes, with *Aipysurus* second (Tables 1.1, 2.1; Figure 2.4). This is true both in Australia and worldwide. However, Australia is relatively poorer in species of *Hydrophis* and relatively richer in *Aipysurus* compared to the world at large. For example, the Australian hydrophiid fauna contains all of the known species of *Aipysurus* but only slightly more than half (52 per cent) of the world's *Hydrophis*. *Aipysurus* accounts for 23 per cent of the Australian species of hydrophiids, compared to 14 per cent of the worldwide hydrophiids.

The tropical north contains the largest density of species of hydrophiids, with 16–17 species occurring per region on the northwestern shelf, Arnhem Land and the Torres Straits (Figure 2.5). When *Acrochordus granulatus* and the local species of homalopsines are added, the number increases to 19–21 species per region.

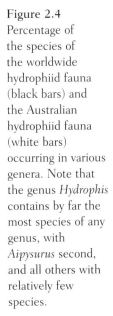

Figure 2.4 Percentage of the species of the worldwide hydrophiid fauna (black bars) and the Australian hydrophiid fauna (white bars) occurring in various genera. Note that the genus *Hydrophis* contains by far the most species of any genus, with *Aipysurus* second, and all others with relatively few species.

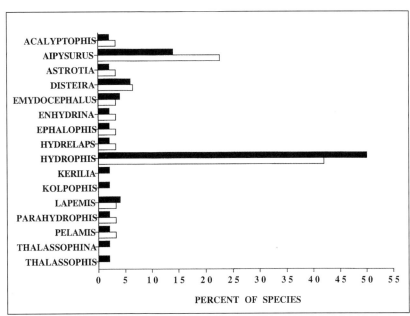

Table 2.1

Characteristics of marine snakes from a variety of localities

Family & Species	Adult Length (cm)*	Habitat & Depth	Food Habits
ACROCHORDIDAE			
Acrochordus granulatus	60 (120) total	Eurytopic; freshwater, reefs intertidal areas, mudflats mangroves; to 20 m	Small fish and crabs
HOMALOPSINAE			
Cerberus rynchops	60 (120) total	Estuaries and mangroves	Crabs and small fish
Fordonia leucobalia	60 (100) total	Mudbanks and mangroves	Crabs and small fish
Myron richardsonii	40 (60) total	Littoral or supra-littoral zones of mangroves and mangrove-lined creeks	Crabs
LATICAUDIDAE			
Laticauda colubrina	75–128 s–v (360 total)	Coral islands, coral reefs, mangroves, the sea	Eels
Laticauda laticaudata	80–96 s–v	Coral islands, coral reefs, mangroves, the sea	Fish
HYDROPHIIDAE			
Acalyptophis peronii	(100) total	Sandy areas on coral reefs	Gobies
Aipysurus apraefrontalis	50 total	Reef flat, reef edge	Eels and possibly other fish
Aipysurus duboisii	70 total	Coral reefs; reef flats to 50 m	Generalised fish eater
Aipysurus eydouxii	100 total	Turbid waters, 30–50 m	Fish eggs
Aipysurus foliosquama	60 total	Reef flats, reef edges; shallows	Fish
Aipysurus fuscus	(60) total	Reef flats, reef edges; shallows	Labrid and gobiid fish
Aipysurus laevis	79–86 s–v (200 total)	Coral reefs	Generalised fish eater
Aipysurus pooleorum	—	—	—
Aipysurus tenuis	—	—	—
Astrotia stokesii	103–141 s–v (200 total)	Turbid coastal water; coral reefs	Fish
Disteira kingii	150 (190) total	Deep water; various substrates	Fish
Disteira major	130 total	Turbid, deep water	Fish
Emydocephalus annulatus	75 (120) total	Shallow water on coral reefs	Fish eggs
Emydocephalus ijimae	57 s–v	—	Fish eggs
Enhydrina schistosa	78–85 s–v (150 total)	Shallow bays and estuaries	Mainly cat fish; other fish; prawns
Ephalophis greyi	50 total	Mangroves; estuarine mudflats	—

Species	Length*	Habitat	Prey
Hydrelaps darwiniensis	50 total	Mangroves and mudflats	—
Hydrophis atriceps	100 total	—	Fish
Hydrophis belcheri	100 total	—	Eels and other fish
Hydrophis brooki	89–92 s–v	—-	—
Hydrophis caerulescens	68–72 s–v	Muddy bottoms?	Bottom-dwelling fish (eels, gobies)
Hydrophis cantoris	116–141 s–v	—	—
Hydrophis coggeri	100 total	Coral reefs and seagrass beds	Eels
Hydrophis cyanocinctus	137–175 s–v		
Hydrophis czeblukovi	120 total	—	—
Hydrophis elegans	170 (200) total	Turbid, deep water; deeper water between reefs	Eels
Hydrophis fasciatus	92–101 s–v	—	—
Hydrophis gracilis	87–93 s–v	—	Fish
Hydrophis inornatus	70 total	—	Fish
Hydrophis klossi	98–119 s–v	—	—
Hydrophis lapemoides	86–87 s–v	—	—
Hydrophis macdowelli	80 total	Turbid estuaries and inshore waters	—
Hydrophis mammilaris	73–76 s–v	—	—
Hydrophis melanosoma	102–111 s–v	Shoal waters	Eels
Hydrophis obscurus	106–109 s–v		
Hydrophis ornatus	78–84 s–v	Eurytopic; coral reefs; turbid inshore waters and estuaries	Fish
Hydropis pacificus	140 total	—	—
Hydrophis spiralis	148–171 s–v (275 total)	—	— —
Hydrophis stricticollis	91–96 s–v	—	—
Hydrophis torquatus	79–81 s–v	—	—
Hydrophis vorisi	60 total	—	—
Kerilia jerdoni	51–53 s–v	—	—
Lapemis curtus	72–83 s–v	Eurytopic; coral reefs to turbid estuaries	Generalised fish eater
Parahydrophis mertoni	50 total	Coastal and estuarine mangroves; mudflats	—
Pelamis platurus	56–66 s–v	Pelagic; surface slicks	Small pelagic fish
Thalassophina viperina	74–83 s–v	—	—
Thalassophis anomalus	67–72 s–v	—	—

* Values are mean lengths of adult snakes with those in parentheses indicating maximum length recorded; where two values are given they represent the mean lengths of the different sexes in species with sexual dimorphism in size. Literature sources vary in the way lengths of snakes are expressed. The most common measurement is from snout to vent (s–v) and when possible that measurement is indicated in the table; however, for some species only total length is known and is so designated.

Note: The species listed cover more than 75 per cent of the world's species of marine snakes. The characteristics of many of the remaining species are poorly known.

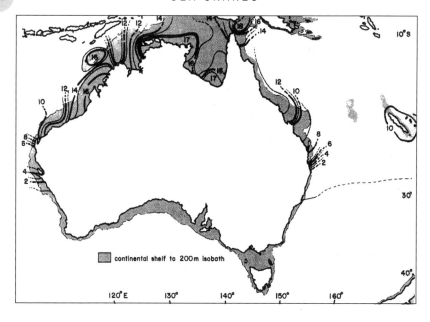

Figure 2.5 Approximate species density of venomous sea snakes in Australian and adjacent waters. Numbers indicate the number of species resident throughout the year in the area subtended by the line associated with the number.

The Great Barrier Reef has 16 species of hydrophiids scattered along its length, with species density gradually decreasing southward to eight at Swain Reefs at the southern end of the outer barrier. South of the Great Barrier Reef, sea snakes soon disappear altogether, with the reefs of Lord Howe Island being completely devoid of them and with the coast of New South Wales having only the pelagic *Pelamis platurus*.

There is a similar decline in species density southward along the western coast of Australia with sea snakes disappearing south of Shark Bay. On both coasts, sea snakes extend south of the Tropic of Capricorn, and thus into the subtropics but reach their winter limit at a latitude of about 25°S.

There are several recurrent patterns of distribution among Australian hydrophiids. These are:

- *Pan-tropical*: Of the 32 Australian hydrophiids, 11 species have distributions covering most of the general range of the family in Australia, that is, stretching from somewhere on the western coast all the way across the northern coastline and then down the eastern coast. These species are: *Acalyptophis peronii*, *Aipysurus duboisii*, *Aipysurus eydouxii*, *Aipysurus laevis* (illustrated in Figure 2.6), *Astrotia stokesii*, *Disteira kingii*, *Disteira major*, *Hydrophis elegans*, *Hydrophis ornatus*, *Lapemis curtus* and *Pelamis platurus*. One species, *Emydocephalus annulatus*, has a similar distribution but with a gap in the Gulf of Carpentaria and part of Arnhem Land.
- *Central Northern*: Seven species range across part or all of the northern part of the country but do not extend down either the

Figure 2.6
Distribution patterns of sea snakes within Australia. Pantropical: *Aipysurus laevis.* Central Northern: *Hydrophis inornatus.* Western Shelf: *Ephalophis greyi.* Torres Straits: *Hydrophis gracilis.* Gulf of Carpentaria: *Hydrophis caerulescens.* (From Cogger 1992)

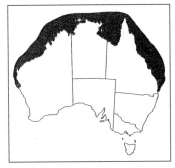

eastern or western coasts. These are: *Enhydrina schistosa, Hydrelaps darwiniensis, Hydrophis atriceps, Hydrophis belcheri, Hydrophis inornatus* (illustrated in Figure 2.6), *Hydrophis mcdowelli* and *Parahydrophis mertoni.*

• *Western Shelf*: Seven species have their ranges in Australia restricted to part of the western shelf. These are: *Aipysurus apraefrontalis, Aipysurus foliosquama, Aipysurus fuscus, Aipysurus tenuis, Ephalophis greyi* (illustrated in Figure 2.6), *Hydrophis coggeri* and *Hydrophis czeblukovi.*

• *Gulf of Carpentaria*: The Australian ranges of two species, *Hydrophis caerulescens* (illustrated in Figure 2.6) and *Hydrophis pacificus,* are restricted to the Gulf of Carpentaria.

• *Torres Straits*: Three species are known in Australia only from the Torres Straits and the tip of Cape York: *Hydrophis gracilis* (illustrated in Figure 2.6), *Hydrophis melanosoma* and *Hydrophis vorisi.* It is curious that there are no species restricted in their distribution to the Great Barrier Reef.

• *Endemic*: Eleven species of sea snakes occur in Australian waters and nowhere else. All of these endemics are hydrophiids. Thus, 34 per cent of Australia's hydrophiids and 29 per of Australia's total marine snake fauna are endemic. Even within Australia some of these endemics have restricted distributions. *Aipysurus apraefrontalis* (Plate 9), *Aipysurus foliosquama* and *Aipysurus fuscus* are known only from Ashmore Reef and a few nearby reefs on the northwestern shelf. *Ephalophis greyi* occurs only in the vicinity of Broome and *Aipysurus tenuis* is found in that locality and in the Arafura Sea. *Hydrophis czeblukovi* is known only from a small area off the northwestern coast and *Hydrophis vorisi* has only been found near the tip of Cape York Peninsula. Several other hydrophiid species, although apparently restricted to the waters bordering

Australia, have wide distributions across the northern part of the country. These include *Acalyptophis peronii*, *Disteira kingii*, *Emydocephalus annulatus* and *Hydrophis mcdowelli*.

Of the hydrophiid species that are not endemic a few have quite limited ranges, such as *Hydrelaps darwiniensis*, known only from northern Australia and southern New Guinea, and *Parahydrophis mertoni* found outside of Australia only in the Aru Islands.

Many of the Australian hydrophiids are widespread elsewhere. Some barely enter Australian waters but have extensive ranges outside the region. Examples are *Hydrophis gracilis* that in Australia is known only from the Torres Straits, yet it occurs otherwise from Indonesia to the Persian Gulf, and *Hydophis caerulescens* that occurs from India to China but in Australia is known only from part of the Gulf of Carpentaria. Other species are common in Australia as well as widely distributed elsewhere. An example is *Hydrophis ornatus* that occurs across northern Australia in habitats ranging from the clear waters of coral reefs to turbid inshore waters and estuaries, and also ranges westward to the Persian Gulf.

Although the laticaudids, as a family, extend from Niue in the southern Pacific Ocean westward to India, and are abundant in some localities in New Guinea, they have been recorded in Australia only from scattered

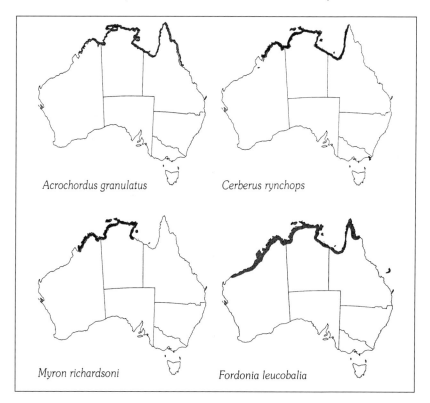

Acrochordus granulatus

Cerberus rynchops

Myron richardsoni

Fordonia leucobalia

Figure 2.7 The Australian distribution of the acrochordid *Acrochordus granulatus* and the homalopsines *Cerberus rynchops*, *Myron richardsonii* and *Fordonia leucobalia*. (After Cogger 1992)

localities as isolated individuals. These probably represent strays from outside the country rather than established Australian populations.

Acrochordus granulatus, the only marine acrochordid, is widespread in the Australasian region. In Australia it has a broadly central northern distribution (Figure. 2.7).

Australia's three species of homalopsines, *Cerberus rynchops, Myron richarsonii* and *Fordonia leucobalia*, all have broadly central northern distributions (Figure 2.7), with the last extending farther down the western coast than most species with this type of distributional pattern.

New Guinea

There are 32 species of marine snakes known from New Guinea, including the country of Papua New Guinea, Irian Jaya and the Aru Islands. Mark O'Shea provided a comprehensive guide to the marine snakes of Papua New Guinea and recognised two laticaudids (*L. colubrina, L. laticaudata*) and 20 hydrophiid species in nine genera, including *Acalyptophis* (*A. peronii), Aipysurus* (*A. duboisii, A. eydouxii, A. laevis*), *Astrotia* (*A. stokesii), Disteira* (*D. kingii, D. major), Enhydrina* (*E. schistosa, E. zweifeli), Hydrelaps* (*H. darwiniensis), Lapemis* (*L. curtus), Pelamis* (*P. platurus*) and eight species of *Hydrophis*. An additional three species of hydrophiids are known from the western part of the island of New Guinea (Irian Jaya of Indonesia) or from the Aru Islands; these are *Emydocephalus annulatus, Hydrophis ornatus ocellatus* and *Parahydrophis mertoni*.

There are six species of homalopsines known from New Guinea, of which two are from fresh water only. The remaining four, although also occurring in fresh water, are primarily from marine or brackish situations. These are *Cantoria annulata, Fordonia leucobalia, Myron richardsonii* and *Cerberus rynchops novaeguineae*.

There are two species of file snakes (family Acrochordidae) in New Guinea, one of which (*Acrochordus granulatus*) occurs in marine habitats as well as in fresh water.

Solomon Islands

Michael McCoy chronicled the snake fauna of the Solomon Islands and listed seven marine species as present: three *Hydrophis*, two *Laticauda* (excluding *L. crockeri* that is restricted to Lake Te-Nggano), *Pelamis platurus* and *Acrochordus granulatus*.

Coral Sea

The northeastern Australian coastal waters have 2–18 species of sea snakes, depending on latitude. Between the localities of Fraser Island and Hinchinbrook Island off the Queensland coast there are 14 species of hydrophiids in nine genera. At about that same latitude but on the outer edge of the Great Barrier Reef and around the islands of the western Coral Sea, the number is reduced to eight species in seven genera. The Chesterfield Reefs in the eastern Coral Sea west of New Caledonia have six known species in five genera. From these data, there seems to be a reduction in diversity from the Australian coast eastward into the Coral Sea. This may reflect the smaller patches of suitable habitat away from the coast rather than merely an eastward decline since numbers of species increase again slightly on the other side of the Coral Sea in New Caledonia.

Other kinds of marine snakes are absent in the Coral Sea except for stray *Laticauda* species.

New Caledonia

New Caledonia has a known hydrophiid fauna of eight species in six genera, slightly more than on Chesterfield Reefs in the Coral Sea to the west. In addition, there are two laticaudids (*Laticauda laticaudata* and *L. colubrina*), making a total of ten marine species. There are no homalopsines or acrochordids.

Vanuatu

Sea kraits are very abundant in Vanuatu, including *Laticauda colubrina* and *L. laticaudata*. A third laticaudid species whose taxonomic relationships are currently under investigation also is found there. The hydrophiid fauna is poorly known but includes at least *Hydrophis coggeri*, *Disteira major* and *Pelamis platurus*; other species almost certainly are present. Thus, there are at least six species of marine snakes in Vanuatu and probably more.

Fiji

Fiji falls within the general geographic range of nine species of marine snakes but Michael Guinea reports only four of these to have been reliably recorded as occurring there; these are two laticaudids (*Laticauda colubrina* and *L. laticaudata*) and two hyrophiids (*Hydrophis coggeri* and the ubiquitous *Pelamis platurus*).

Tonga

Tonga has two resident species of laticaudids, *L. colubrina* and *L. laticaudata*. A third laticaudid also has been listed as a vagrant.

Niue

Niue, a self-governing nation on an island of only 259 square kilometres in the Pacific Ocean about a third of the way from Tonga toward the Cook Islands, is the easternmost limit (longitude 170°W) of laticaudids. Michael Guinea reviewed the marine snake fauna of Niue and reported two species, *Laticauda schistorhyncha* and *Laticauda laticaudata*. No hydrophiids have been reported from Niue but it lies within the general range of *Pelamis platurus* and that species may well occur there.

PHILIPPINES

Edward Taylor gave an early report of the snakes of the Philippines that later was supplemented by William Dunson and Sherman Minton. After accounting for nomenclatural differences, the total fauna of 15 marine snakes is now known to include one acrochordid (*Acrochordus granulatus*), two homalopsines (*Cerberus rynchops* and *Fordonia leucobalia*), three laticaudids (*Laticauda colubrina, L. laticaudata, L. semifasciata*) and nine hydrophiids. The latter include five species of *Hydrophis* and one species each from the genera *Aipysurus, Astrotia, Lapemis* and *Pelamis*.

TAIWAN

Shou-Hsian Mao and Been-Yuan Chen summarised the Taiwanese sea snake fauna as consisting of seven native species, of which three are laticaudids and four are hydrophiids. The former are *Laticauda laticaudata, L. colubrina* and *L. semifasciata*. The latter are *Emydocephalus ijimae, Hydrophis melanocephalus, H. cyanocinctus* and *Pelamis platurus*. They also considered three other species (*Lapemis curtus, Astrotia stokesii* and *Hydrophis ornatus*) as strays probably brought by currents from the mainland; however, these may merely be relatively rare, native species.

CHINA

According to Zhao Er-mi and Kraig Adler, the marine snake fauna of mainland China includes *Acrochordus granulatus*, three laticaudids (*Laticauda laticaudata, L. coubrina, L. semifasciata*) and 13 hydrophiids, of which six species are in the genus *Hydrophis* (*H. caerulescens, H. cyanocinctus, H. fasciatus, H. gracilis, H. melanocephalus, H. ornatus*). Other hydrophiids are *Emydocephalus ijimae, Acalyptophis peronii, Astrotia stokesii, Lapemis curtus, Thalassophina viperina, Kerilia jerdonii* and *Pelamis platurus*. Two Chinese homalopsines enter salt water (*Enhydris bennetti* and *E. chinensis*). This gives a total marine snake fauna of 19 species.

JAPAN

Michihisa Toriba reviewed the sea snake fauna of Japan and reported nine species. One of those, *Lapemis curtus*, probably occurs only as strays drifting in on currents from further south, and is not represented by breeding populations in Japanese waters. The eight native species include five hydrophiids (*Emydocephalus ijimae, Hydrophis ornatus, H. melanocephalus, H. cycnocinctus* and *Pelamis platurus*) and three laticaudids (*Laticauda semifasciata, L. laticaudata, L. colubrina*). All of these occur mainly in the tropical waters of the Ryukyu Islands, with records from the main islands of Japan (mostly of *P. platurus*) probably representing strays transported by currents.

CHAPTER 3

NATURAL HISTORY

Natural history encompasses the vital activities of a species, where it lives, how it behaves, how it grows and reproduces, the stages through which it passes during its life and how it perceives its environment. These general topics are covered in this chapter. In later ones some topics of natural history, such as feeding, defence and adaptation to the marine environment, are treated in more detail.

GENERAL HABITAT

Marine snakes occupy a great diversity of habitats. Some species are eurytopic, that is, they occupy a wide range of habitats and occur at a variety of depths and in situations ranging from muddy, turbid water to the clear waters of coral reefs. For example, *Acrochordus granulatus* occurs in fresh water as well as in salty places, such as mudflats, mangrove swamps and coral reefs, and has been found in the sea as far as 10 kilometres offshore and at depths as great as 20 metres. *Astrotia stokesii* (Figure 3.1) and *Lapemis curtus* (Plate 11) also occur in many situations. However, other species have narrower ecological requirements and are restricted to particular habitats such as coral reefs (*Emydocephalus annulatus*), shallow estuaries (*Enhydrina schistosa*),

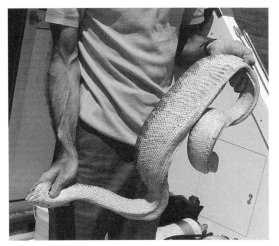

Figure 3.1
The author holding
Astrotia stokesii
(family
Hydrophiidae), one
of the most massive
species of sea
snakes. Note the
flat ribbon-like
body. This species
is widely distrib-
uted in Australian
and southeastern
Asian waters but
usually it is not
very abundant.
(Photograph
courtesy of
Ben Cropp)

muddy bottoms (various *Hydrophis* species) mangroves (several homalopsines) or saltmarshes (some races of *Nerodia*).

Depth may be an important factor. *Disteira kingii* and a number of species of *Hydrophis* seem to be found only in deep water, whereas other species, such as some *Aipysurus*, are found chiefly in shallow water. In general, the genera *Aipysurus* and *Emydocephalus* seem to be limited to a water depth of 50 metres or shallower whereas some other hydrophiids occur in water twice that deep.

Some species occupy deeper water in some parts of their range than in others. For example, *Hydrophis coggeri* was the species at Ashmore Reef that fed at the greatest depth (50 metres) whereas in Fiji it was commonly found in seagrass beds or even up creeks, in water as shallow as one metre. A summary of the habitat of Australian marine snakes appears in Table 2.1.

A major difference in habitat between the sea kraits (laticaudids) and true sea snakes (hydrophiids) is the degree of restriction to aquatic habitats. Hydrophiids are entirely marine and never voluntarily leave the water whereas laticaudids regularly come out onto land (Plate 7), either to lay eggs or to rest or to digest a meal among crevices in rocks or under debris on the shore.

Temperature may limit the kinds of habitats sea snakes can occupy. Most species live in warm tropical to subtropical waters (see Chapter 2) and seem unable to persist indefinitely elsewhere. Although individuals may be carried into cool regions such as Tasmania or New Zealand and survive for some time, they do not reproduce under those conditions and breeding populations cannot become established.

Except for the temperate American natricines from saltmarshes and estuaries, no sea snakes occur in the Atlantic region and none occur in the Caribbean. Four to five million years ago the isthmus of Panama was open and there was a Pacific–Atlantic connection. It is likely either that hydrophiids had not yet reached the western coast of the Americas before that avenue for dispersal closed or that there were ecological barriers to dispersal through the connecting waterway. The cold water off the southern tip of Africa and along the southwestern coast of South America may constitute present-day barriers to dispersal. *Pelamis* reaches the eastern coast of Africa and the western coast of the Americas but has never succeeded in rounding the capes of either continent to gain access to the Atlantic (Figure 2.2). When there were plans for a sea-level canal in Panama (since abandoned), there was concern that *Pelamis* would be able to move through it from the eastern Pacific Ocean and invade the Caribbean Sea.

BODY SIZE

Most species of sea snakes average between half a metre and a metre in total length when adult but maximum sizes often exceed a metre. Several species reach larger sizes, with average body length of adults exceeding a metre and maximum lengths reaching two metres (Table 2.1). The longest hydrophiid probably is *Hydrophis spiralis* at 2.75 metres for unusually large individuals; among the laticaudids, giant *Laticauda colubrida* have been recorded at lengths of up to 3.6 metres.

Most species of marine snakes are slender but *Astrotia stokesii* is massively built (Figure 3.1). Although growing on average to only about 1.2 metres in total length, it has a large girth and is the bulkiest of the marine snakes. An individual of 1.6 metres in length and about 3 kilograms in weight was reported to have a girth of 28 centimetres. *Acrochordus granulatus*, the homalopsines and the saltmarsh natricines are all of modest size, most having an average adult size of about half a metre in body length, with a maximum size of slightly more than a metre.

SEXUAL DIMORPHISM

In reptiles generally sexual dimorphism in body size seems to be the rule rather than the exception, with it favouring one sex about as often as it does the other. However, snakes in general may differ from other taxa of reptiles. In 66 per cent of 224 species of snakes (all kinds), females were larger than males. The value just for sea snakes is similar. Of the 29 species of marine snakes for which there are relevant data, 19 species (66 per cent) have females larger than males, eight species (28 per cent) have males larger than females and in two species (7 per cent) both sexes are approximately the same size (Table 3.1). The three species of laticaudids for which data are available are all sexually dimorphic in favour of females. Similarly, the homalopsine *Bitia hydroides* has larger females than males.

Sometimes sexual dimorphism in body size is very marked. For example, female *Laticauda colubrina* grow a third longer than do males, despite males having longer tails. In *Aipysurus laevis* not only are females longer than males but for a given length, they are heavier.

There is also sexual dimorphism in the number and character of scales. Some *Laticauda* species show sexual dimorphism in the number of rows of dorsal scales and in the number of subcaudal scales. Male *Lapemis* species have larger spines on their body scales than do females.

Table 3.1

Sexual dimorphism and clutch size of some marine snakes

Species	Sexual Dimorphism*	Clutch Size
ACROCHORDIDAE		
Acrochordus granulatus	—	(4.3; 4.8; 4.9); 1–12
HOMALOPSINAE		
Bitia hydroides	F > M	(4.2)
Cantoria spp.	—	6–8
Cerberus rynchops	—	8–26
Fordonia leucobalia	—	13
Gerarda prevostiana	—	5
LATICAUDIDAE		
Laticauda colubrina	F > M	up to 18
Laticauda laticaudata	F > M	7
Laticauda schistorhyncha	F >M	3
Laticauda semifasciata	F > M	(3.9)
HYDROPHIIDAE		
Acalyptophis perionii	—	up to 10
Aipysurus eydouxii	—	(4.4)
Aipysurus laevis	F > M	(2.6); 2–5
Astrotia stokesii	F > M	12–14
Emydocephalus ijimae	F = M	—
Enhydrina schistosa	F > M	(18.3); 4–11
Hydrophis brooki	M > F	(4.9); 7
Hydrophis cuerulescens	M > F	(5.9); 2–6
Hydrophis cantoris	F > M	6
Hydrophis coggeri	—	1–8
Hydrophis cyanocinctus	F > M	3–16
Hydrophis fasciatus	M > F	(3.3); 2–4
Hydrophis gracilis	F > M	1–16
Hydrophis klossi	F > M	—
Hydrophis lapemoides	M > F	2–5
Hydrophis mammilaris	F > M	4
Hydrophis mcdowelli	—	2–3
Hydrophis melanocephalus	F > M	—
Hydrophis melanosoma	—	(6.0)
Hydrophis obscurus	F > M	5–10
Hydrophis ornatus	M > F	—
Hydrophis spiralis	F > M	5–14
Hydrophis strictocolis	F > M	9
Hydrophis torquatus	M > F	(5.5)
Kerilia jerdoni	F > M	3–4
Lapemis curtus	F = M	(3.3); 1–6
Pelamis platurus	F > M	(3.6); 2–6
Thalassophina viperina	M > F	(3.5); 3
Thalassophis anomalus	M > F	5

* F = female; M = male.

Note: Multiple values given in the third column are derived from different literature sources. Where means were given they are listed in parentheses in the table; the values not in parentheses are ranges.

REPRODUCTION AND DEVELOPMENT

COURTSHIP AND MATING

Like all snakes and lizards, male marine snakes have two copulatory organs. They were not given full credit as separate penises by the original describer but rather were called *hemipenes* or half-penises. In fact, each one is a fully functional unit and during any given mating only one of them is used. Hemipenes are bag-like and lie in individual sheaths, one on either side of the base of the tail just behind the vent. During mating, the one to be used is everted through the opening of its sheath and turned inside out. It is covered by an array of spikes and hooks (Figure 3.2) that help keep it in place during mating (Plate 15). A groove, which serves as a channel for the transfer of sperm runs along the ventral border. When disturbed during copulation, the larger female often flees, dragging the hapless, smaller male along by the hemipenis (Plate 16).

Mating is sustained for long periods and spans more than one breathing cycle. During mating the female controls the breathing rhythm, surfacing when she needs air; the male must try to gulp air at the same time or do without until the next cycle as he is unable to disengage until mating has been completed.

Courtship has been observed in only a few species. In *Aipysurus laevis* the prelude to mating consists of the male swimming in an exaggerated sinuous way above the female, occasionally nipping at her neck. Males of the turtle-headed sea snake (*Emydocephalus annulatus*) have a spine on the tip of the snout (Plate 10) with which they prod the head and neck of the female during courtship.

Reptiles have two major modes of reproduction. Some lay eggs and are called *oviparous*. Other species give birth directly to live young and are called *viviparous*. In many oviparous species the eggs are retained for some time in the mother's body where development of the embryo begins. When the egg subsequently is laid, the time until hatching is reduced by the extent that internal development has taken place. The length of time the egg is retained and the proportion of development

Figure 3.2
Hemipenes of laticaudid snakes.
A. *Laticauda colubrina*.
B. *Laticauda laticaudata*.
C. *Laticauda crockeri*.
D. *Laticauda semifasciata*.
Note the groove on the underside that carries sperm during mating. (From Cogger et al. 1987)

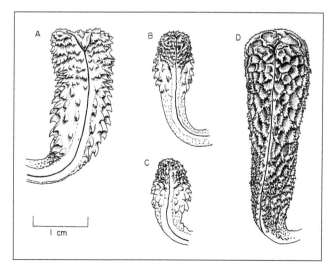

that takes place internally varies from species to species and provides a continuum from no internal development to retention for the entire embryonic period. So there is a gradual evolutionary transition from egg-laying to live-bearing. At the latter extreme, the egg shell no longer forms. The acrochordids, homalopsines, *Nerodia* species and the hydrophiids are all viviparous and the laticaudids are egg-layers.

Marine snakes carry their eggs or young further forward in the body than do viviparous land snakes. This is probably a reflection of the fact that extra weight in the back of a marine snake's body would interfere with swimming movements; young in that position in land snakes would not greatly affect locomotion.

VIVIPARITY

Figure 3.3
The left reproductive tract of a female olive sea snake (*Aipysurus laevis*) showing two large yolk-filled eggs. (Photograph courtesy of Glen Burns)

The young of viviparous snakes are well supplied with yolk which they use as nourishment during their development (Figures 3.3, 3.4, 3.5, 3.6, 3.7).

Gestation time in some marine snakes is longer than for most terrestrial species. For examples in *Aipysurus laevis* gestation takes nine months, in *Acrochordus granulatus* it takes 11 months; and in *Cerberus rynchops*, six months. An exception is *Enhydrina schistosa* which, like most viviparous land snakes, has a gestation period of three to four months.

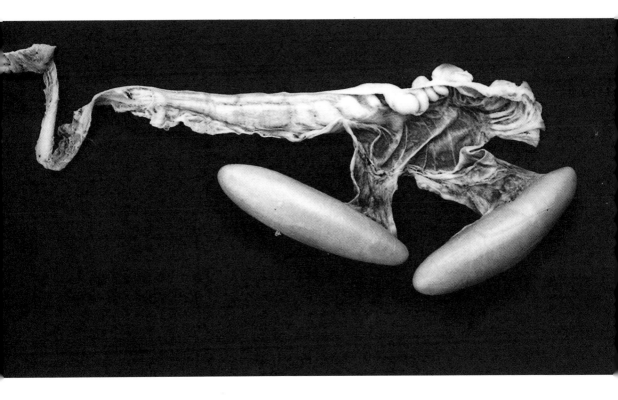

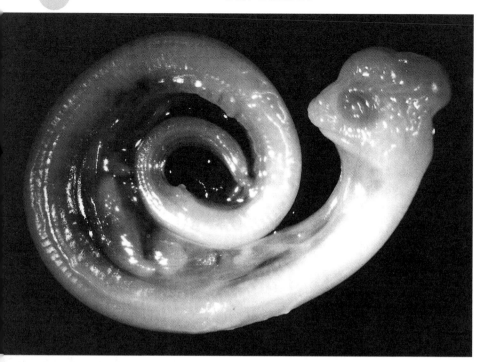

Figure 3.4
An early embryo of
the olive sea snake
(*Aipysurus laevis*).
(Photograph
courtesy of Glen
Burns)

Figure 3.5
Later embryo of
the olive sea snake
(*Aipysurus laevis*).
(Photograph
courtesy of
Glen Burns)

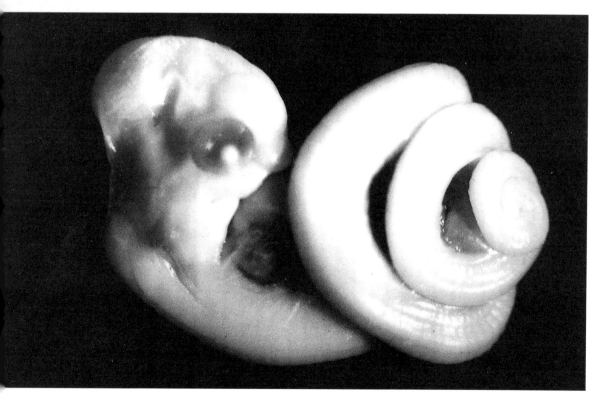

Figure 3.6
An embryo of the olive sea snake (*Aipysurus laevis*) at about mid-gestation. (Photograph courtesy of Glen Burns)

Figure 3.7
Full term embryo of the olive sea snake (*Aipysurus laevis*). Note juvenile colour pattern. (Photograph courtesy of Glen Burns)

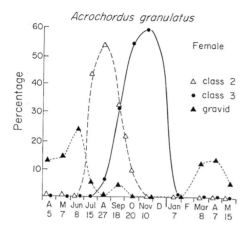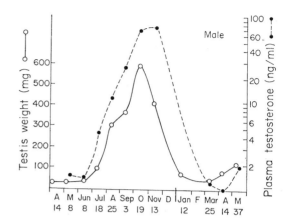

The young of viviparous sea snakes are born underwater. Soon after, they surface for their first breath and from then on they lead an existence independent of their mother. There is no parental care.

OVIPARITY

Like sea turtles, and unlike most sea snakes, the sea kraits are oviparous and leave the water to lay eggs on land. There may be one exception. *Laticauda crockeri*, a lake-locked species in the Solomon Islands, is said by local people to be a live-bearer. Their other observations on the natural history of this species were accurate and their opinion should not be taken lightly. Two expeditions to Lake Te-Nggano, the home of this species, failed to find a gravid female so the problem remains unresolved. If it is viviparous, it is the only laticaudid to be so.

REPRODUCTIVE CYCLES

Although almost all marine snakes are tropical to subtropical, some breed only during a short period of the year. For example, *Hydrophis coggeri* has a brief (two-month) breeding period. In the Philippines, three sympatric species show different seasonal patterns of reproduction. *Laticauda colubrina* breeds aseasonally, the homalopsine *Cerberus rynchops* is loosely seasonal and the acrochordid *Acrochordus granulatus* breeds synchronously and is highly seasonal (Figure 3.8). *Laticauda semifasciata* has a prolonged breeding season in Taiwan.

Female *Aipysurus laevis* on the Great Barrier Reef exhibit synchronous seasonal reproduction with ovulation occurring in spring. Embryonic development occupies about nine months and parturition occurs in autumn. This gestation period is long compared to those of most terrestrial snakes and it is likely that individual females require an

Figure 3.8
Reproductive cycle of female (left) and male (right) *Acrochordus granulatus* in the Philippine Islands. For females the percentages represent the proportion of the individual females that contain reproductive products of the following classes: Class 2 = follicles of 5–15 mm in diameter, Class 3 = heavily yolked follicles of 15–30 mm in diameter; gravid means carrying embryos. Testosterone is the male sex hormone. (From Gorman et al. 1981)

intervening non-breeding summer in order to replenish exhausted energy reserves. This accords with the observation that in this species individual females probably only breed every second year. *Acrochordus granulatus* also has a long gestation time (5–8 months) that is associated with females breeding at longer than yearly intervals. At the other end of the scale, the oviparous *Laticauda semifasciata* probably breeds more than once per year.

In a study of 14 species of marine snakes along the Malaysian coast, it was found that snakes at some localities had tightly synchronised annual reproductive cycles but at other places even the same species had less precise cycles or bred aseasonally. *Bitia hydroides*, an homalopsine, had a strongly seasonal reproductive cycle but was out of phase with sympatric hydrophiids. A given species may vary from one extreme to the other at different localities. *Acrochordus granulatus* in the Philippines has a well-defined seasonal breeding cycle whereas in the Straits of Malacca it is aseasonal. *Laticauda colubrina* is aseasonal in the Philippines but seasonal in Fiji. So even such a basic characteristic as reproductive cycle may show marked geographic variation.

GROWTH

Data on the growth of sea snakes are scanty. Harold Voris and his co-workers studied the beaked sea snake (*Enhydrina schistosa*) in Malaysia and found growth to be 1.6 per cent per day (0.5 g per day or 1.2 mm in body length per day) (Figure 3.9).

Glen Burns, in a study of the olive sea snake (*Aipysurus laevis*) on the Great Barrier Reef recorded growth rates of 2.2–9.5 millimetres per month, with the higher rates occurring among the younger animals. Growth rate declined abruptly at the attainment of sexual maturity. *Lapemis curtus* grow at a rate of 1.0 millimetre per day. Growth rates of 0.3–0.5 millimetres per day have been reported for other species.

ATTAINMENT OF SEXUAL MATURITY

Other attributes being equal, snakes that grow rapidly and reach sexual maturity early will be able to replenish population losses more quickly than slower-growing species or those that reach maturity later.

In *Aipysurus laevis* males reach sexual maturity in their third year and females in their fourth or fifth year. This is later than is true for their closest terrestrial relatives, the Australian elapids, that require only 12–31 months, depending on the species, to reach sexual maturity. By contrast, age of sexual maturation of some other sea snakes fall within the range for Australian elapids e.g. *Enhydrina schistosa*: 1.5 years and

Laticauda colubrina: 1.5 years for males and 1.5–2.5 years for females. The homalopsine *Bitia hydroides* in Malaysia reaches sexual maturity at an age of one year, twice as early as sympatric hydrophiids.

ACTIVITY PERIOD

Some species of sea snakes seem to be nocturnal (active by night) and others are mainly diurnal (active by day). One, *Aipysurus duboisii*, has been reported to be crepuscular (active during the twilights of dawn and dusk). However, many do not restrict their activity to particular portions of the day.

Sea snakes appear to sleep. Although they lack eyelids and cannot close their eyes, motionless snakes on the bottom sometimes appear to be startled, as though awakened, when touched. Nevertheless, periodically they must swim to the surface to breathe and cannot remain completely inactive for longer than their breath-holding ability allows.

Round-the-clock activity for some species extends beyond the mere requirements of surfacing to breathe. Underwater observations and sonic tracking of *Aipysurus laevis* revealed that the same individual snake foraged for food during both day and night. Captive animals of that species in a large cement tank showed no marked differences in activity levels between night and day.

By contrast, some species show consistent daily cycles in the frequency with which they appear on the surface. For example,

Figure 3.9
Growth of the beaked sea snake (*Enhydrina schistosa*, family Hydrophiidae) in Malaysia. Note that after sexual maturity females grow larger than males. s indicates the standard deviation. (From Voris and Jayne 1979)

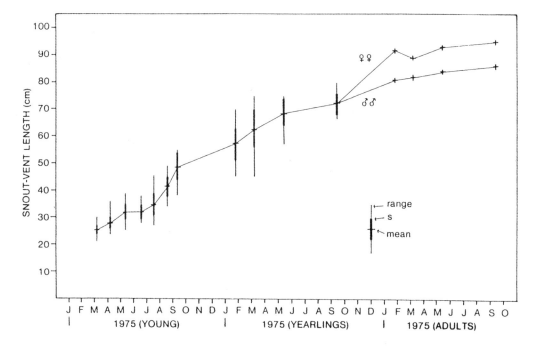

night-time netting at the surface in the Philippines caught several species of *Hydrophis* that were not caught by day but yielded only a few individuals of other species, such as those of *Laticauda*, that were observed by day and known to be locally abundant. It is not clear whether these observations reflect overall activity patterns or merely that active snakes spend different proportions of time on the surface at different times of day. The underwater activity cycle of these species is unknown.

Other cycles may be of more importance than the diel (day–night) one. The beaked sea snake (*Enhydrina schistosa*) is active either by day or by night but is inhibited in its activity at those stages of the tidal cycle when strong currents are running. In some cases a combination of diel and tidal cycles may be important for particular activities. *Laticauda colubrina* moves between land and sea primarily during nocturnal high tides.

MOVEMENTS

Many species of sea snakes are widely dispersed and must have crossed areas of deep water unsuitable for their permanent occupancy, either by active migration or by being passively carried by currents. The latter certainly has happened on a number of occasions and nearly dead sea snakes (especially *Pelamis platurus*) may be found far outside their usual geographic range after severe storms.

A spectacular aggregation of sea snakes in the Malacca Straits was reported in 1932 by Willoughby Lowe. From the deck of a ship he observed a nearly solid mass of a species reported to be *Astrotia stokesii* in a line about three metres wide and 100 kilometres long, containing literally millions of snakes, many intertwined with each other. Such an event certainly is not a regular feature of the biology of any sea snake and it is not known whether it was a migration or some other phenomenon. It may have been a passive aggregation of these animals in a slick during unusually calm or 'oily' conditions, such as regularly occurs on a smaller scale in the suface-inhabiting *Pelamis platurus*.

Some regular migrations have been chronicled, although not quantified. *Laticauda* seems to aggregate in particular localities at certain times of year. Also, it has been reported that in southeastern Asia and northern Australia sea snakes of various species move inshore and then retreat seaward again on a regular basis, depending on their reproductive cycles and upon seasonal changes in currents and in productivity of inshore waters. This postulated movement, although probably true, requires more rigorous documentation.

Figure 3.10
Freeze-branding a sea snake, *Aipysurus laevis*, with a permanent number. (Photograph by the author)

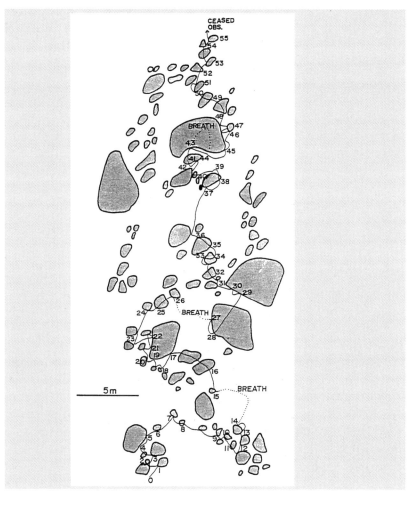

Figure 3.11
Path of a foraging adult *Aipysurus laevis* at Mystery Reef, Swain Reefs, Great Barrier Reef, Queensland, Australia. Dark areas are coral heads (bommies) and white represents sand. The solid line tracks the foraging snake with numbers indicating successive minutes. Dotted lines represent surfacing for a breath. The snake slowly foraged in crevices in the coral but swam rapidly over open sand. (From Burns and Heatwole, 1998)

Figure 3.12
Home ranges of the
olive sea snake
(*Aipysurus laevis*) at
Passage Rocks,
Keppel Islands,
Great Barrier Reef,
Queensland,
Australia. Above:
Photograph of part
of a reef at Passage
Rocks, showing the
home range of an
ultrasonically
tracked adult
female. Numbers
indicate locations of
a snake over succes-
sive days, with the
suffixes a (morning)
and b (afternoon or
night) indicating
different locations
on the same day.
Below: Maps of the
home ranges of
seven ultrasonically
tracked adults
(individuals A–G).
Note that the
home ranges of dif-
ferent individuals
overlap broadly.
(From Burns and
Heatwole, 1998)

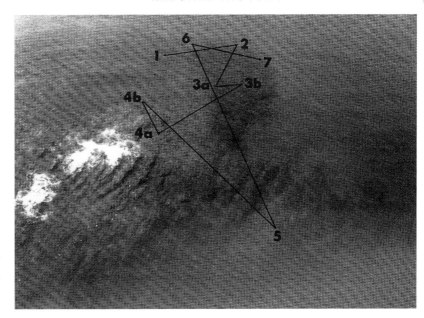

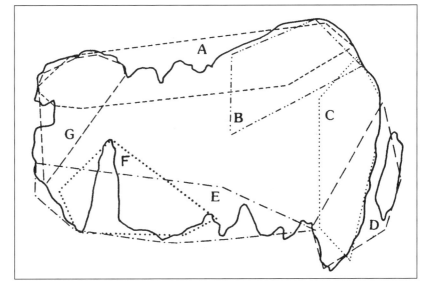

Whatever the overall situation, it is certain that some species are remarkably restricted to a small local area much of their life. The observation that in the Swain Reefs on the Great Barrier Reef certain patch reefs were teeming with olive sea snakes (*Aipysurus laevis*), whereas similar ones nearby lacked snakes, and that these differences persisted year after year, prompted me and one of my PhD students, Glen Burns, to study the distances individuals moved. We perma-nently numbered snakes by freeze-branding them (Figures 3.10 and

Plate 17) and recording where they were subsequently found. For tracking over shorter periods, we put a small transmitter into a recently killed fish and then hand-fed the fish to an unmolested foraging snake in its natural habitat. The ultrasonic sounds produced by the transmitter could be lowered to a range audible to humans by an underwater receiver with headphones. We used this apparatus to locate snakes repeatedly (Plate 18) and to follow them and plot their successive positions on a map of the reef (Figure 3.11).

We found that olive sea snakes have a definite home range, that is a definite area to which they confine their activities. The home ranges of individual snakes varied from 0.15 to 0.18 hectares (Figure 3.12) and thus were smaller than the home ranges of many species of land snakes. When snakes whose home range had been mapped in an area of coral were moved across a sandy channel only about 200 metres wide, they did not return.

Lack of movement across even narrow barriers of unsuitable habitat means that unoccupied reefs may remain unpopulated by this species for a long time, being colonised only by the action of a storm or other infrequent event that tranports snakes from a nearby inhabited reef.

The home ranges of different individuals overlapped broadly but snakes were never observed to defend any part of their home ranges against other individuals of the same species. Therefore it appears that they are not territorial.

SENSORY PERCEPTION

Except for some burrowing species that have reduced eyes and poor eyesight, terrestrial snakes are highly visual and can recognise prey by sight. They also have a good olfactory sense. They extend the tongue (Plate 19) and airborne chemicals dissolve in its moist membrane. When the tongue is retracted, a sensory pit, called the Jacobson's organ, in the roof of the mouth detects the odours. They can use this sense of smell to follow the trail of prey or a potential mate, even when they have lost visual contact. Some snakes have heat-sensitive areas in the scales of the upper lip (pythons) or concentrated in a pit on the side of the face (rattlesnakes and their relatives). Using these stereo heat-detectors, snakes can detect and accurately strike warm prey in complete darkness.

Sea kraits and true sea snakes have Jacobson's organs and use their tongues to assist olfaction in the detection and identification of prey but do not have heat-sensitive organs. They have well-developed eyes and can see objects at a distance; curiously, they seem unable to use vision in the recognition of prey.

Figure 3.13
Five zones (I–V)
of the tail of
Aipysurus laevis
showing the
per cent of
stimulations by
light that resulted
in movement of
the tail out of the
light. Some of the
scales are shown
for reference.
Note that the
upper surface of
Zone II near the
tip of the tail is
most sensitive to
light. (From
Zimmerman and
Heatwole 1990)

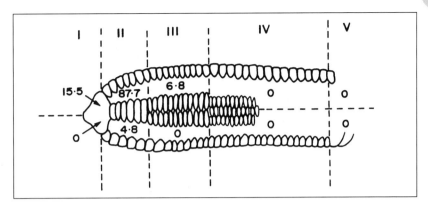

Sea snakes do have a light-sensitive capability so far not found in any land snake. Kenneth Zimmerman and I noticed during many dives that during the day the tails of olive sea snakes (*Aipysurus laevis*) seldom were seen protruding from the cover of coral in which they were resting but that at night they were exposed frequently. We discovered that when a light was directed onto the tail, 78 per cent of the time the snake would move it out of the beam but when the head or mid-body was illuminated, movement away from the light only occurred 2–4 per cent of the time. After over 350 such casual observations, we decided to conduct a more rigorous experiment and we directed a small beam from a fibre-optic light onto small areas of the tail. Only the tip of the tail was sensitive, and the upper surface was much more sensitive than the lower one (Figure 3.13). Placing black plastic film over the light-sensitive areas abolished the response. The likely function of this caudal photosensitivity it that the snake can detect when its tail is under cover and the snake completely concealed from predators.

Freshwater and estuarine races of *Nerodia* differ in their drinking of salty water and David Zug and William Dunson set out to ascertain the sensory organs used to detect salinity. They eliminated involvement of the tongue and Jacobson's organ in the detection of salt and suggested that taste, located in papillae in the mouth, might be responsible.

CHAPTER 4

FOOD AND FEEDING

Many predators use their limbs to run down their prey and to grasp, kill and dismember it once it is caught. Being limbless, snakes cannot avail themselves of these techniques and yet many, including most sea snakes, are successful predators upon agile prey. This chapter portrays how they forage for food and what they eat.

FORAGING AND CAPTURE OF PREY

Four methods of foraging for food and catching prey have been described for marine snakes. The most common type is 'crevice-foraging'. Crevice-foraging is employed by file snakes, sea kraits and many species of hydrophiid. The snakes swim slowly near the bottom, periodically protruding their tongues against the substrate and poking their heads into crevices or holes (Plate 20). When suitable prey is detected — probably by smell via the tongue (see pages 44–45) — it is quickly bitten and then swallowed. In some cases it is released but the snake attends it until it dies, at which point it is consumed. Snakes have been observed taking captured prey to the surface or swallowing it there; however, on most occasions swallowing takes place on the bottom. I have seen olive sea snakes (*Aipysurus laevis*) going completely around

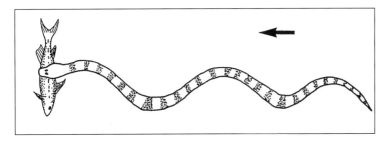

Figure 4.1
Method of capture and swallowing of prey by *Enhydrina schistosa* (family Hydrophiidae). A fish encountered while the snake is swimming is struck and retained until it ceases struggling (upper); then it is manipulated so the snake can find the head end, and the fish is swallowed head-first. During the initial states of swallowing (lower), the snake swims with its head facing posteriorly, using the water current to keep the fish aligned. Arrows indicate direction of movement of the snake. (Modified from Voris et al. 1978)

the perimeter of a recently killed fish, touching the edges with their tongues as though measuring its size before beginning to ingest it. This species of snake also has been observed quickly wrapping itself around a piece of coral in which prey has been discovered, effectively sealing off escape routes with the body and tail. Similarly, *Acrochordus granulatus* encloses its prey within folds of its body, thereby blocking escape.

The second method of foraging is 'cruising near the bottom'. This has been described by Harold Voris and his colleagues in detail for the beaked sea snake (*Enhydrina schistosa*). The snake swims slowly just above the bottom and when either bumping directly into a fish or coming within a few centimetres of it, it strikes laterally by opening its mouth and rapidly swinging its head sideways. Misses are common. The prey is held at whatever part of the body is bitten at the instant of strike and the grip is maintained until the victim ceases struggling. Meanwhile the snake swims forward using the pressure of the water against the prey to help hold it in its mouth (Figure 4.1). Once the prey is incapacitated it is positioned for swallowing. The snake accomplishes this by releasing its grip for an instant and then re-gripping at a different point, gradually moving toward the head end. If erect pectoral spines are encountered, it may atttempt to go around the other way or to rotate the fish to avoid the spines. When the head is reached swallowing begins.

During the initial stages of swallowing, the snake turns its head toward the tail (the 'J-position') and swims with the loop of the neck in the direction of movement (Figure 4.1). Water flow helps keep the fish properly aligned.

Some *Hydrophis* also seem to capture food in this way but differ in that they consume still-struggling eels. Heroic contests sometimes develop, perhaps a reflection of the fact that some eels are remarkably resistant to venom and are difficult to subdue (see page 107).

A third type of prey-capture, 'ambush', is known only in the yellow-bellied sea snake (*Pelamis platurus*). This species floats at the surface in slicks. Small fish often occur there, either as surface-active schools or as individuals seeking shelter beneath floating objects in the drift line. When such fish approach *Pelamis* closely, they are struck by a sidewise motion of the snake's head; if they are located behind the snake's head, the strike is accompanied by the snake swimming backwards. This species is unusual in being able to swim either forwards or backwards equally well, merely by reversing the direction of movement of its lateral undulations.

Finally, *Emydocephalus annulatus*, because of its specialised diet, feeds in an unusual way that has been observed by Michael Guinea. This species has an expanded second supralabial scale on its upper jaw (Plate 10) that it uses as a blade to scrape the sticky eggs of damselfish from the coral branches where the fish deposit them. The fish guard their eggs and sometimes are able to prevent the snakes from getting them.

Regardless of the method of capture, most sea snakes swallow prey head-first. Were it swallowed tail-first, the sharp spines of the dorsal and pectoral fins would be forced into the erect position and would either catch in the jaws or lodge in the throat, thereby preventing further swallowing and perhaps injuring or killing the snake. When swallowing is head-first the spines fold backward against the fish's body, offering less resistance and reducing the likelihood of injury. Even so, there are some injuries from spines. Sea snakes are sometimes found with fish spines embedded in their body wall from the inside; in one case a stout spine was firmly lodged in the skull of a snake with the tip protruding from the top of its head.

Vision seems to play little part in the capture of prey by any of the three methods. Snakes can capture fish equally well in the dark or in the light, and some species forage nocturnally. No sea snakes are known to actively pursue swimming prey. Often fish are ignored even when they pass only a few centimetres from a snake's head. When snakes lose a fish, they frequently are unable to find it again even when it is well within visible range. Sea snakes have good vision (see page 44, sensory perception) but they do not seem to be able to process visual input centrally in a way that permits identification of prey.

The two senses that seem to be most important in feeding are olfaction and sensitivity to small water currents caused by the movement of fish. The tongue is an organ mediating smell and its use during foraging suggests it may be important in identifying prey that are touched or cornered in crevices. If the water is permeated with fish juice and its source is not readily associated with any object, snakes become highly motivated and less discriminating. Finely chopped fish dropped in an aquarium induces a 'frenzy' in *Pelamis platurus* and any object encountered, including another snake, is bitten.

Movement of fish near a snake's head can initiate a strike, even if the tongue has not contacted it. Also, vibration of an inert object (such as a pair of forceps) near a *Pelamis platurus* can stimulate it to turn toward the source of the vibration, move toward it with its mouth open and eventually bite. Vibration of a dead fish near a *Pelamis platurus* causes it to approach. If it contines to be vibrated the snake can find it. If it is held still, the snake often cannot locate it.

In summary, it would appear that most hydrophiids and laticaudids do not visually search for prey. Odour and water vibrations can stimulate foraging behaviour. The former may also facilitate identification of prey and initiate striking; the latter may direct the snake toward its prey as well as stimulate striking.

Although response to odour and water vibrations explain most of the feeding responses of sea snakes, other senses may be involved in a lesser way. Gentle tactile stimulation on the body of *Pelamis platurus* causes it to swim backwards and strike. Snakes have oral papillae that probably are taste organs and may aid in detecting whether objects grasped in the mouth are suitable prey.

Feeding by one marine homalopsine, the bockadam (*Cerberus rynchops*) was studied by Bruce Jayne and his colleagues. This species actively strikes a swimming fish, rapidly moves the prey back to the corners of the mouth, flexes the neck and holds the fish perpendicular to the snake's neck (Figure 4.2). When struggling by the fish ceases or is reduced, the snake holds onto the fish and 'walks' its jaws around the periphery of the prey until the head is reached. Then the fish is swallowed head-first (Plate 2). The larger the fish or the greater its struggling, the longer the snake held it before attempting to swallow it. This delay allows time for the toxic saliva to penetrate the wound and immobilise the prey (see Chapter 9).

Striking by the homalopsine *Cerberus rynchops* seems to be induced by a combination of olfactory and tactile stimuli. When fish odour is present in the water, this species strikes in the direction of disturbances in the water simulating fish movements.

Many natricines seem to use vision in hunting and the saltwater races of *Nerodia* employ active pursuit of small fish, especially those trapped in small pools by the tide.

The hypodermic-like fangs of hydrophiids

Figure 4.2
Capture of prey by *Cerberus rynchops* (subfamily Homalopsinae). The diagram is based on tracings from successive video frames. The dotted line indicates the earlier position in each pair of tracings.

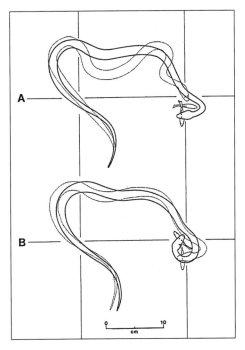

and laticaudids are used to inject venom into live prey (see Chapter 9). The rows of solid teeth behind the fangs hold prey during swallowing. These teeth are recurved and once a victim is impaled, escape becomes very difficult. The only way to get free of a tooth is to move in the direction toward the throat. Escape from one tooth merely means the next one behind obtains a grip.

Snakes have flexible skulls. Some of the bones are not tightly bound into a rigid framework but rather can move relative to each other. Because of this, the snake can bite down on one side of its head and hold its prey, while the bones on the other side lift up and disengage the teeth, then move them forward for a new purchase. The two sides of the head hold and move forward alternately and 'walk' their way over the prey, pulling their gape around the victim. The lower and upper jaw can disengage and the skin of the head and throat distends allowing the passage of very large prey.

Some sea snakes have been known to consume eels that are longer than themselves. Others commonly take prey twice the diameter of their own head (see Chapter 9). Large prey cannot gain complete entry into the snake's stomach immediately. Consequently, fish taken from sea snake stomachs often have the head end well digested but the tail relatively intact. Usually only one fish is found inside a snake. Exceptions are *Pelamis platurus* and *Acrochordus granulatus* in which a meal may consist of many small fish.

It is likely that the predilection of many sea snakes for eels or other elongate fish may be because they fit better into a snake's body and a larger meal can be consumed. Even with snakes' prodigious ability to swallow large objects, there is a limit to the diameter of fish that can pass through the jaws. An eel of the largest diameter that a snake can swallow weighs a lot more and provides a much larger meal than a fish of the same diameter but of more globular shape.

DIET

The dietary habits of Australian marine snakes are summarised in Table 2.1).

Despite the similarity in foraging modes of many bottom-dwelling snakes, the food that different species eat sometimes varies widely, even in the same locality. Part of this dietary variability may reflect differences in habitat or microhabitat. For example, snakes foraging in holes in the sand would obtain different kinds of fish (e.g. gobies) than would those nearby foraging in crevices in coral. However, the causes of dietary differences go beyond that. In some cases, there is selection of only certain kinds of fish. In laboratory tests where a choice of prey is offered, the beaked sea snake (*Enhydrina schistosa*) eats certain species in preference to others, those selected being the ones most commonly occurring in the stomachs of these snakes when captured in the field.

I studied the feeding of two species of sea kraits that live in Lake Te-Nggano in the Solomon Islands. Both forage in the same places, at the same times of day and in the same manner (crevice-foraging). I saw two individuals, one of each species, investigating the crevices in the same sunken log within minutes of each other. There are only two native species of fish in the lake: an eel and a gudgeon (*Eleotris fusca*); an introduced species, *Sarotheradon mossambicus*, is not eaten by either snake. One species of snake, *Laticauda colubrina*, eats only the eel, while the other, *Laticauda crockeri*, eats only the gudgeon. Both species of fish are sedentary. Clearly, this is a case of preference for one food type over another. The diet of *Laticauda colubrina* also has been studied by various biologists in different parts of its range, including New Guinea, Fiji and New Caledonia. In all these places, its diet consists almost entirely of eels.

Hydrophiids and laticaudids fall roughly into one of two feeding categories: the specialists and the generalists. Generalists eat fish of many species and from a number of families (in some cases over 20), as well as invertebrates such as squid, cuttlefish and crabs. However, they do not exploit the full range of fish in their habitat as the sensory capabilities and methods of foraging of some species restrict them to the more sedentary or crevice-inhabiting prey. Fast-swimming pelagic fish are less often included in the diet, although *Aipysurus laevis* and *Lapemis curtus* eat some relatively active species. These probably are captured during the prey's inactive period when they have retreated to crevices, the nocturnal species being captured by day and the diurnal ones by night.

In contrast to a small number of generalists, there are many food specialists among sea snakes (Table 2.1, page 22). The type of fish on which they specialise are mainly sedentary ones, especially those that inhabit crevices or live in burrows.

Eels and gobies are the most common specialities (Figure 4.3). The genus *Hydrophis* contains several species with extremely small heads and long, thin necks that connect to a much stouter body; they feed exclusively on eels that live in deep burrows in the mud. So the peculiarly narrowed anterior ends of these snakes is probably an adaptation allowing them to penetrate the narrow burrows of their prey. Some of the more conventionally shaped *Hydrophis*, as well as *Laticauda colubrina*, also are eel specialists.

The most highly specialised feeders among sea snakes are those that eat fish eggs almost exclusively. There are only three species that have such a restricted diet: *Aipysurus eydouxii* and the turtle-headed sea snakes (*Emydocephalus annulatus* and *E. ijimae*). They forage on corals and among crevices and burrows, as do many other sea snakes. Often they accidentally ingest considerable amounts of sand along with their meal of eggs, a practice that must influence their buoyancy.

The diet of the granulated file snake (*Acrochordus granulatus*) in marine habitats consists mainly of crevice-inhabiting or sedentary fish such as gobies, blennies and mudskippers. Crustaceans and snails also have been reported as dietary items for this species.

The homalopsines that live in salt water feed mainly on fish and crabs. *Fordonia leucobalia* and *Myron richardsonii* seem to especially favour crabs. *Bitia hydroides* in Malaysia eats mainly gobies, as do hydrophiids from the same locality.

The saltmarsh natricines eat mainly small fish but fiddler crabs have also been reported. In the fresher waters of their habitat they also may eat frogs.

Figure 4.3
The number of sea snake species preying on fish of different body shapes. The numbers inside the bars indicate the number of families of fish of that shape. (From Voris and Voris 1983)

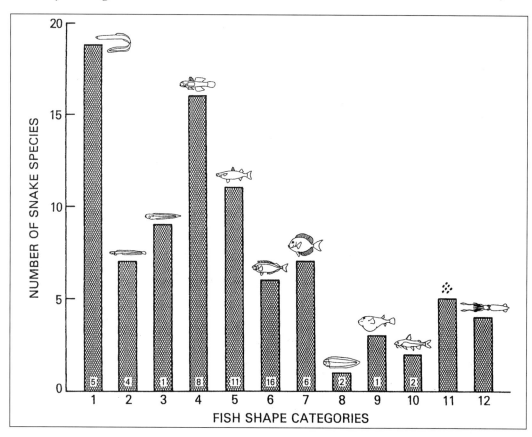

ENEMIES

The web of life has many links and practically every species is at risk of being devoured by another species, either by direct attack or, more subtly, by the gradual consumption of small animals within. It is a constant struggle to eat but not be eaten. Sea snakes are top predators, yet they have their enemies. This chapter introduces those enemies.

PREDATORS

Venomous animals such as hydrophiids and laticaudids might be expected to have few enemies. Indeed some species of sea snakes are avoided by potential predators and can go about their daily lives relatively immune from attack. The yellow-bellied sea snake (*Pelamis platurus*) seems to be one such species. It is contrastingly coloured, the underside being bright yellow and the back black, with conspicuous yellow and black markings on the tail; such bold colouration in the animal kingdom often signals a warning to would-be predators that the object of their attention has noxious qualities and would be better left alone.

A search through the stomachs of many predatory fish from areas where *Pelamis platurus* are abundant has not revealed any predation upon them. Frigatebirds have been seen to pick up *Pelamis platurus* from the surface of the sea but drop them again.

Ira Rubinoff and Chaim Kropach conducted experiments in marine tanks that showed that a variety of predatory fish, including sharks, not only did not attack *Pelamis platurus* but usually refused its meat, even when skinned, cut into pieces, coloured differently or sandwiched between pieces of squid which they do accept. On the few occasions when such deceptions were successful and the fish ate the meat, it was usually regurgitated.

The above results were obtained using fish collected from waters where *Pelamis platurus* is abundant (Pacific coast of Panama). An interesting difference in response occurred when fish from the Atlantic side (where sea snakes do not occur) were used instead. Some fish attacked and ate the snakes and of those, some were bitten by the snakes and died. In one case a snapper swallowed an individual *Pelamis platurus* and died an hour later, in the meantime having regurgitated its meal. It is not known whether the differences in predatory behaviour among fish from the two waters is because of learning from individual experience or because natural selection in the Pacific has favoured the trait of rejecting *Pelamis platurus*.

Paul Weldon conducted a series of experiments to identify the cues predators use in recognising and rejecting *Pelamis platurus*. He found that pieces of their meat with the skin attached frequently were rejected by snappers, even in the dark, and that when pieces were eaten they often were regurgitated. When different body parts were offered separately, the skin was found to be eaten less often and regurgitated more frequently than skinned meat. Pieces of palatable fish meat treated with extracts from the skin of *Pelamis platurus* were regurgitated. Although it is likely that in nature this species is identified and rejected on the basis of a combination of criteria, probably including visual and mechanical cues, it is clear that there are chemicals in its skin that act as a deterrent to predation.

Despite the large measure of protection enjoyed by *Pelamis platurus*, it is not complete. There are two known cases of natural predation on this species: once by a pufferfish and once by a leopard seal. The latter was outside its usual range; it was ill, perhaps because of having eaten the snake. Both animals regurgitated the snakes they had consumed. In captivity, an octopus ate a *Pelamis platurus*, an unlikely event in nature. Billfishes have been observed striking this species and knocking them out of the water but have not been observed eating them. A small proportion of *Pelamis platurus* bear scars on their bodies that resemble scratches such as might be made by birds or they have pieces missing from their tails, that look like bite marks. Crabs will scavenge upon dead *Pelamis platurus*.

Non-venomous marine snakes and even many venomous ones lack the degree of protection from predation afforded to *Pelamis platurus.* Sea eagles (*Haliastur indus* and *H. leucogaster*) are known to eat sea snakes. I collected the remains beneath an eagle perch at One Tree Island on the Great Barrier Reef. Sea snakes were included among the food scraps, along with a variety of fish, sea birds, cuttlefish and crabs.

Sharks are also important predators. I examined the records of stomach contents of over 7000 sharks obtained from the netting of bathing beaches in Queensland. Six of the 19 species of sharks involved were found to have eaten sea snakes. In most of these the incidence of predation was low. The exception was the tiger shark (*Galeocerda cuvieri*) which regularly eats sea snakes; in some cases as many as four were found in a single stomach. From those localities where sea snakes occurred in some abundance, 5–33 per cent of the tiger sharks had snakes in their stomachs. Other predators such as moray eels, groupers, sweetlips and other fish, as well as saltwater crocodiles, have been reported eating hydrophiids.

Predators upon marine snakes are not limited to vertebrates. Crabs may be an important predator on some species. Michael Guinea noted that a portunid crab attacked and ate a live sea krait (*Laticauda colubrina*). Harold Voris and William Jeffries examined the gut contents of the common mangrove crab (*Scylla serrata*), and found that 5 per cent of the stomachs contained snake scales or vertebrae. In captivity, this crab readily captured and ate the dog-faced water snake (*Cerberus rynchops*), an homalopsine species.

PARASITES

Most vertebrates have their complement of parasites on their skin and in their body cavities, blood, internal organs and digestive tracts. This aspect of sea snake biology has not been studied very extensively but enough is known to indicate that, like other reptiles, hydrophiids have a variety of parasites. There are nematodes in the guts of many. Almost all of the olive sea snakes (*Aipysurus laevis*) collected on the Great Barrier Reef have worms in the lungs. Two species of lung mites are known from sea snakes. About 9 per cent of the *Lapemis curtus* from the Gulf of Carpentaria contained a species of trematode in the stomach.

Parasites on the outside of the body (ectoparasites) are not present on many species of hydrophiid. Most of the organisms that attach externally, such as barnacles, algae and bryozoans (see page 56, Fouling Organisms), do not extract nourishment from the snake and so are not parasitic.

Laticaudids commonly have a species of tick, *Amblyomma nitidum*, that is restricted to them, never having been found on any other kind of animal. There is also a report of another species of tick, usually found on terrestrial reptiles, occurring on a sea krait. Several species of chigger mites (family Trombiculidae) also infest species of *Laticauda*. Ectoparasitic ticks and mites characteristically attack terrestrial animals and the semi-terrestrial habits of laticaudids probably account for their infestations by such parasites.

FOULING ORGANISMS

Like other snakes, marine snakes periodically shed their skins. Just before shedding is due the skin loosens and an oily secretion forms between the old and new layers, including the scale over the eye. Accordingly, the snake becomes duller in colour and the eye appears cloudy (Plate 21). Snakes often become relatively inactive at this time.

It was once thought that marine snakes shed their skin piecemeal but now it is known that at least some shed it whole, just as do land snakes. The snake rubs its lips against a piece of coral or other hard object to loosen the skin, then catches it against some protrusion to anchor it and work it free. It then crawls out through the old mouth, leaving the skin turned inside-out behind it (Plate 21).

Sea snakes shed rather frequently —at 2–6 week intervals — probably more often than required by growth alone. Part of the function seems to be to rid the snake of marine organims that grow on its skin.

Barnacles, bryozoans and algae are all fouling organisms on sea snake skin. The barnacles *Platylepas ophiophilus* and *Octolasmis grayii* have been found only on sea snakes. The number of barnacles on any one snake is usually low and many snakes are entirely free but infestations of up to nearly 600 individuals have been reported. Most are sloughed with the old skin but in one case 74 of 75 individuals survived shedding and remained attached to the snake. The barnacles receive protection from predation, as well as an increased food supply brought to them in the currents passing over the moving snake. They provide no benefit to the snake and their only harm seems to be minor damage to the skin.

Many marine snakes have a few patches of algae on their skin and in some cases a rather heavy growth (Plate 22). These do not seem to harm the snake and are invariably lost during shedding.

Pelamis platurus, being a surface-dweller, does not have access to solid objects to assist it in shedding. It has the unusual habit of coiling itself into knots and rubbing the coils against each other as the body is drawn through in the tying and untying process. This behaviour seems to assist shedding and shed skins often have one or more overhand knots in them (unlike those of other species). Knotting may also serve to scrape fouling organisms off the skin.

POPULATION AND COMMUNITY ECOLOGY

Population biology, or demography, treats the fluctuations in numbers of individuals of a species at a particular place. Usually an attempt is made to assess the relative contributions of birth rates (natality) death rates (mortality) and immigration and emigration of individuals to those fluctuations. The structure of the population in terms of the relative numbers of different genders, ages (sizes) and reproductive status are important parameters in understanding changes in the numbers of animals per unit area (population density).

POPULATION DENSITY

There have been few estimates of population densities of marine snakes. Glen Burns, one of my PhD students, and I used freeze-branding to mark individuals of *Aipysurus laevis* (Figure 3.10, page 42) along 3000 metres of reef edge at Mystery Reef, Great Barrier Reef and obtained population estimates of 2100–2806 snakes or 0.70–0.94 snakes per metre of reef edge. These snakes were much less abundant over the reef flat or over sandy habitats abutting the reef.

Harold Voris and his colleagues have studied populations of marine snakes at various localities in Malaysia. They estimated that there were approximately 1–3 adults of the homalopsine *Cerberus ryn-chops* per metre of shoreline at one locality. At another place, an estu-ary, they estimated the population of *Enhydrina schistosa* to be 900–1400 juveniles and 1300 adults.

Densities of *Laticauda colubrina* were estimated by Hubert Saint Girons to be 4.9/m² for one small island in New Caledonia and sev-eral thousand snakes on an area of 2000–3000 m² on another one. A small island in Malaysia had 791 resident snakes of this species. The high densities of *Laticauda* in these studies represent concentrations at resting sites; *Laticauda colubrina* ranges over a much wider area of reef in search of food.

The factors influencing the densities of sea snakes are poorly understood. Some patch reefs have dense populations of *Aipysurus laevis* whereas nearby ones that otherwise appear similar are devoid of snakes; similarly, some small islands host dense aggregations of *Laticauda* species and others in the same area do not.

SEX RATIO

Sex ratio is the proportion of males and females in the population, with 1:1 indicating an equal number of males and females. The observed sex ratio of sea snakes varies from locality to locality and at a given place from one occasion to another. Cliff Leman and Harold Voris found that among 622 embryos from 38 gravid females of *Enhydrina schistosa*, the sex ratio was not significantly different from equality. Thus, at birth the sex ratio in this species is even. Later it may be altered, perhaps by different levels of mortality among females and males. Alternatively, and more likely, males and females may occupy somewhat different microhabitats or have different activity levels that make them differentially susceptible to capture, without there actually being a preponderance of one sex over the other.

By contrast, the sea krait, *Laticauda colubrina*, has a sex ratio that is skewed toward males. The bias toward males occurs among young snakes and becomes more pronounced in the adult size classes. In *Laticauda semifasciata* the sex ratio is skewed toward males (64 per cent), even in hatchlings.

The apparent sex ratio in *Aipysurus laevis* alters during the year in ways that may reflect seasonal changes in behaviour. Most courtship and mating takes place in winter (July–August). Consequently, the prepon-derance of males at that time may be because they are actively searching for females and hence more conspicuous. Similarly the overall sex ratio in *Lapemis curtus* is nearly 1:1 but there are temporal departures from it that may be related to seasonal changes in reproductive behaviour.

FECUNDITY

Sea snakes have low potential production of young (fecundity) compared to many marine animals and even compared to many terrestrial snakes. Almost half of the species of hydrophiids and laticaudids have a clutch size, that is number of eggs or young produced, of less than five, and about 90 per cent have a clutch size of less than ten. There are a few species with a relatively high fecundity, such as *Astrotia stokesii* with 12–14 young and *Enhydrina schistosa* with an average clutch size of 18.3 (Table 3.1, page 33).

Cliff Lemen and Harold Voris studied the reproduction of 14 species of Asian sea snakes (hydrophiids and *Acrochordus granulatus*). They found that the average clutch size varied among species from 2.9–18.3, with most species bearing between three and six young. In fact the only species in their study with an average clutch size greater than six was *Enhydrina schistosa*.

Four different studies of *Acrochordus granulatus* converged to give a clutch size of 1–11 (average 4.8–4.9).

Homalopsines give birth to 3–21 live young at a time, with numbers reported for the marine species usually being less than ten (Table 3.1). Only *Fordonia leucobalia* and *Cerberus rynchops* have a reported range extending above that value.

The saltwater races of *Nerodia* usually have 2–15 young, although higher values have been reported.

Clutch sizes in marine snakes do not reach the highest values for viviparous land snakes, some of which have broods up to 100; however, relatively few species of land snakes have broods larger than 15.

Two of the oviparous laticaudids, *Laticauda laticaudata* and *L. colubrina*, tend toward larger clutch sizes than any of the hydrophiids except *Enhydrina schistosa* (Table 3.1). Clutch size in *Laticauda*

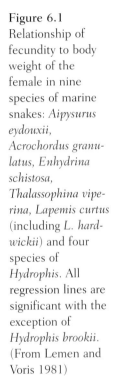

Figure 6.1
Relationship of fecundity to body weight of the female in nine species of marine snakes: *Aipysurus eydouxii, Acrochordus granulatus, Enhydrina schistosa, Thalassophina viperina, Lapemis curtus* (including *L. hardwickii*) and four species of *Hydrophis*. All regression lines are significant with the exception of *Hydrophis brookii*. (From Lemen and Voris 1981)

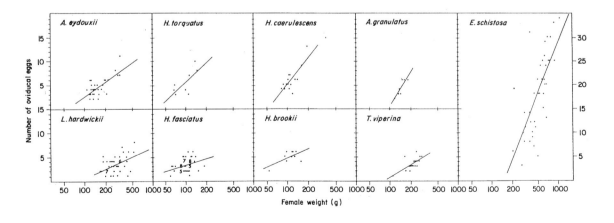

colubrina has been reported to be 4–10 in Fiji and 14–20 in New Caledonia, and so may vary geographically. Only *Laticauda semifasciata* has small clutches. Some oviparous land snakes have small clutches of 3–15 eggs but others lay as many as 45.

Richard Shine from Sydney University recorded where eggs or embryos were located in the bodies of gravid snakes and found that sea snakes carried their young further forward than did land snakes. The fact that extra weight in the back of the body may adversely affect locomotion in sea snakes may limit the proportion of the body cavity that can be used for storage of eggs or embryos and impose a restriction on clutch size apart from other biological considerations.

As in many kinds of animals, fecundity of sea snakes varies with the body size of the mother (Figure 6.1), larger females having a greater number of eggs in their oviducts than smaller animals. Larger females may produce more young because there is more room in a large body for eggs than there is in a smaller one, as long as the size of the eggs are the same in large and small mothers. However, in sea snakes, the matter is more complicated than merely the physical amount of space involved. For example, in *Enhydrina schistosa* the sizes of eggs and young are not the same throughout the size range of females. Large females tend not only to produce a greater number of eggs in the oviducts but those eggs, and the embryos resulting from them, are larger than is true of smaller females. In some other species of sea snakes, the eggs of females of different sizes do not differ.

The relationship between female body weight and clutch size varies among species of sea snakes. In some species large and small females produce clutches of nearly the same size, whereas in other species large females have many more young in a clutch than do small females. A measure of how much clutch size increases for a given increase in female body weight is the slope of the line in a graph relating these two variables (Figure 6.1). A slope of zero means there is no increase in clutch size with increase in female body weight and the flatter (more nearly horizontal) the line, the smaller is the effect of female body size on clutch size. A very large slope with the line inclined more steeply upward means that even a small increase in size of mother results in a substantially greater number of young in a clutch. For example, in Figure 6.1 note that in *Enhydrina schistosa* the number of oviducal eggs increases greatly in larger mothers (strongly inclined line; slope = 35.4) whereas maternal size has much less effect in *Hydrophis fasciatus* (less steeply inclined line; slope = 4.3).

Relative fecundity (brood size divided by total length of female) has been noted to be higher in aquatic and burrowing snakes than in terrestrial or arboreal ones, although no marine species were included in that analysis.

FERTILITY

Fecundity of sea snakes often is determined by counting the number of large-yolked eggs in the oviduct. However, this estimate of clutch size does not take into account the number of those eggs that are infertile.

Fertility is the number of offspring that are produced alive. In the ten species of sea snakes for which data are available, fertility ranged from 80 per cent to 95.5 per cent. That is, of the mature eggs produced, 4.5 per cent to 20 per cent of them are infertile and the energy invested into their production is wasted. The proportion of breeding females that had at least one infertile egg ranged from 5.9 per cent to 59.5 per cent.

REPRODUCTIVE EFFORT

A female can expend either a little or a lot of energy and materials, such as yolk, in producing her offspring. A measure of the magnitude of this expenditure is the total weight of eggs or young produced, expressed as a percentage of the female's body weight without eggs or young. This measure is called reproductive effort.

Cliff Lemen and Harold Voris set out to find out whether marine snakes (hydrophiids and acrochordids) differed in reproductive effort either from land snakes or among themselves, and if so, in what ways. They found that reproductive effort was remarkably constant among the species of sea snakes they studied, with the weight of the whole clutch ranging between 23.6 per cent and 38.9 per cent of female body weight, a difference of only 1.7 fold. However, the same reproductive effort can be achieved either by packaging a few large eggs into the space available or by using the same space for a larger number of smaller eggs, as mentioned before. Various intermediate conditions are also possible. The option of a few large eggs means that the total reproductive effort is channeled into only a few young and consequently the reproductive effort per embryo is much higher than when a greater number of smaller eggs is produced. As a result, although the total reproductive effort is similar among various species of sea snakes, the reproductive effort per embryo differs more widely.

In the ten species of sea snakes for which there are data available the mean reproductive effort per embryo varies from 2.1 per cent (*Enhydrina schistosa*, with an average of 18.3 eggs per clutch) to 10.9 (*Hydrophis fasciatus* with 3.3 eggs per clutch). This represents more than a five-fold difference in reproductive effort per embryo.

Except for *Enhydrina schistosa*, which has a value similar to many

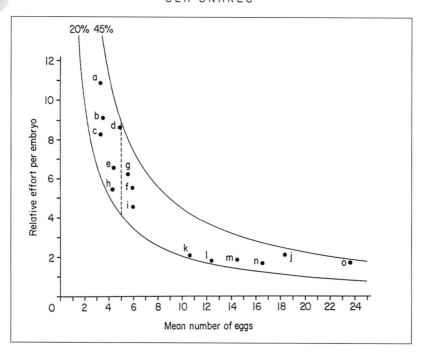

Figure 6.2
Comparison of the
relationship of repro-
ductive effort per
embryo to clutch size
in marine and terrestri-
al snakes. Curved lines
indicate the 20 per
cent and 45 per cent
contours for the rela-
tive effort per clutch.
Species a–j are marine
(all are family
Hydrophiidae except
Acrochordus which is
family Acrochordidae):
a = *Hydrophis fasciatus,*
b = *Thalassophina
viperina,*
c = *Lapemis curtus,*
d = *Hydrophis brookii,*
e = *Aipysurus
eydouxii,* f = *Hydrophis
caerulescens,*
g = *Hydrophis torquatus,*
h = *Acrochordus granu-
latus,* i = *Hydrophis
melanosoma,*
j = *Enhydrina schistosa.*
Species k–o are ter-
restrial: k = *Coluber
constrictor* (Colubridae),
l = *Pseudechis porphyri-
acus* (Elapidae, semi-
aquatic, freshwater),
m = *Thamnophis
sirtalis* (Colubridae),
n = *Austrelaps superba*
(Elapidae),
o = *Notechis scutatus*
(Elapidae).
(From Lemen and
Voris 1981)

land snakes, the reproductive effort per embryo generally is higher in sea snakes than in land snakes (Figure 6.2). This means that most sea snakes tend to invest a greater amount of energy into each of their young but that in consequence they produce fewer of them. Tropical marine habitats may be an unusually hostile environment for small snakes (mortality is high among young sea snakes; see page 63, Mortality and Longevity) and perhaps the larger a newly born snake is, the better chance it may have of surviving. This may be the advantage of producing larger young, even if it means that there are fewer of them.

SIZE STRUCTURE

Several species of marine snakes (*Aipysurus laevis, Laticauda colubrina, Cerberus rynchops*) have small numbers of juveniles in the population relative to adults. This is partly the result of low fecundity and perhaps high juvenile mortality. However, sometimes juveniles may not be as scarce as they appear. On the Great Barrier Reef young *Aipysurus laevis* were seldom observed, even on reefs where adults were abundant. When small snakes were seen, they were usually surfacing to breathe and were not foraging. Perhaps they avoid predation by foraging under the cover of coral rather than in the open, and because of that are hard to find. A similar paucity of young in a population of the homalopsine *Cerberus rynchops* was attributed in part to births occurring in a different habitat or perhaps to weak seasonality in breeding. The only sea snake in which juveniles have been known to rival adults in abundance is *Enhydrina schistosa*. Again this may be an artifact. The estuary being sampled was believed to be a nursery with adults only entering it to breed.

MORTALITY AND LONGEVITY

Mortality can be very high in marine snakes, especially among young individuals. In *Enhydrina schistosa* only 10–20 per cent of the newborn survive the first year and only 6 per cent of females survive to reproduce.

Most longevity records of reptiles are based on captive animals and may not be relevant to field populations; however, some land snakes have been known to survive up to 18 years in the wild, comparable to the longevity of 15 years reported for *Aipysurus laevis* on the Barrier Reef. *Enhydrina schistosa* lives to an age of four years or older, although the older age classes make up only a tiny fraction of the total population.

ASSEMBLAGES OF SEA SNAKES

A biotic community is made up of all of the animals, plants and micro-organisms that live together and interact with each other. Those members of the community that belong to the same taxonomic group make up an assemblage. Thus, within a marine biotic community, there is a fish assemblage, an algal assemblage, a mollusc assemblage, and so on, often including a snake assemblage. Different species in an assemblage use available resources in different ways and the degree of overlap in requirements among them varies. Three categories of potential or actual overlap frequently are deemed of especial importance: the use of food, the use of space and the use of time. Although the topic is controversial, competition for these resources often has been viewed as determining the structure of an assemblage by controlling which combination of species can live together.

Some marine communities have snake assemblages of up to a dozen species, sometimes including hydrophiids, laticaudids, homalopsines and acrochordids. These assemblages do not seem haphazard ones, dependent merely upon the chance association of species that happen to concide in their habitat selection. Rather, it appears that only certain types of combinations occur, and that within those assemblages the species are ecologically segregated, that is they differ in the use of at least one of these three major kinds of resources. The use of food and the use of space stand out as particularly important.

Harold Voris analysed one such assemblage and found that if two species have very similar diets and specialise on the same kind of prey, they usually have different spatial requirements and occupy different microhabitats. Conversely, species that occupy the same place do not depend on the same type of food. It appears that snake assemblages cannot contain specialists that share both diet and microhabitat. They seem to be able to overlap broadly in one or the other resource, but not in both (Figure 6.3). The above remarks apply particularly to food specialists. It is curious that marine snake assemblages can accomodate a generalist that has an overlap in diet with a specialist. The generalist may eat eels, gobies, catfish, as well as other fish not consumed by any specialist. By eating a wide variety of species, it does not consume large numbers of the food supply of any specialist. Although generalists may overlap with specialists, two generalists do not seem to be able to coexist in the habitat. A typical assemblage contains one generalist superimposed upon a series of specialists. Duplication in any of these roles only seems possible if different microhabitats or habitats are occupied.

Why such a pattern should emerge is not entirely clear. Perhaps two species that depend almost entirely on the same kind of prey compete with each other and the one best suited to a particular habitat may eliminate its competitor. The reverse outcome may occur in a different habitat where the rival may have a competitive advantage. Another hypothesis is that previous selection for characteristics reducing competition resulted in evolution of different habitat preferences.

Figure 6.3 Overlap of Malaysian sea snakes in diet and locality. Note that snakes with high overlap in diet rarely occur together in the same localities. The exception is *Lapemis hardwickii* (including *H. curtus*) which overlaps in diet and habitat with many species; it is a generalist (see page 50, Ch 4, Diet). Initials across the top refer to the species listed down the side. (Modified from Voris and Voris 1983)

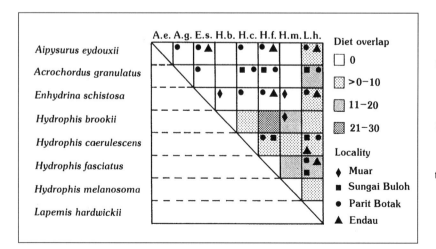

The study of assemblage structure in other groups of animals has shown that in some cases competition is operative but that in others different factors are more important. Detailed studies of the ecology of component species and the way in which they interact are necessary before the competitive hypothesis can either be accepted or discarded for sea snake assemblages. Additional studies are required before it is even known whether the structuring described above applies to marine snake assemblages generally or only to the few that have been investigated so far.

An assemblage is said to be highly equitable if most of its species are of about the same commonness or rarity, that is, all species are represented by about the same numbers of individuals. By contrast a highly inequitable community is one in which the disparity between the rarest species and the most common ones is very great. Often there are only one or two very abundant species but many rarer ones. Few assemblages of marine snakes have been studied in sufficient detail to quantify equitability. However, Robert Stuebing and Harold Voris did so for the assemblage of the western coast of Sabah, Malaysia. That assemblage was highly inequitable, with *Lapemis curtus* accounting for more than three-quarters of all of the snakes and the second most abundant one accounting for only 6 per cent of the total snakes (Figure 6.4). So there was only one superabundant species and nine rarer ones, two of which (*Hydrophis spiralis* and *Laticauda colubrina*) were exceedingly rare, accounting for only one individual each in a sample of over 2000 specimens. This does not mean that the rare species were rare everywhere, only in the habitat being studied. Marine snake assemblages may also be relatively inequitable in Australia. In the Gulf of Carpentaria 53 per cent of all snakes caught by research trawlers were *Lapemis curtus* and in a different part of the Gulf the most abundant species (25 per cent) caught by commercial trawlers was *Hydrophis elegans*.

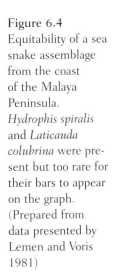

Figure 6.4 Equitability of a sea snake assemblage from the coast of the Malaya Peninsula. *Hydrophis spiralis* and *Laticauda colubrina* were present but too rare for their bars to appear on the graph. (Prepared from data presented by Lemen and Voris 1981)

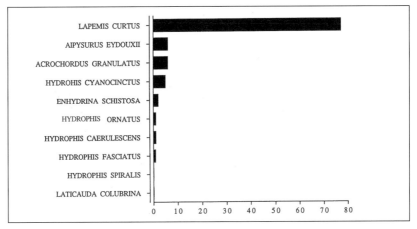

ADAPTATION TO LIFE IN SALT WATER

The sea is an unusual environment for reptiles. Of the approxmately 5300 known species of living reptiles, only about 73 (1.4 per cent) live in a marine or brackish habitat. These include six species of sea turtles, two species of brackish water or saltmarsh turtles, two salt-water crocodiles, the marine iguana lizard and 70 species of snakes (see Chapter 1). Snakes alone have only a slightly higher representation in salty water (2.8 per cent of the approximately 2500 living species). Clearly modern reptiles as a group have not adapted readily to marine conditions and it is of especial interest to examine how the few successful marine taxa cope with such a novel reptilian habitat.

There are several fundamental challenges that the sea poses for animals with a basic reptilian lifestyle and physiology. Salt is in excess and fresh water virtually non-existent. How do sea snakes get rid of excess salts or prevent entry of salts into their bodies? How do they obtain fresh water and conserve it for their vital functions?

Certain amounts of salt and water are needed by all organisms for their life processes. Too much or too little of either results in the inability of an animal to function properly and eventually causes its death.

To understand salt and water balance in sea snakes, a simple physical model can be considered. If two solutions of salt are separated by a membrane that allows the passage of water but not of salt then water will move into the saltier solution from the weaker one: a process called osmosis. This movement of water will continue until the saltiness of the solutions on both sides of the membrane is the same.

The body fluids of sea snakes are not as salty as sea water and so if the skin were a membrane such as described above, one would expect that water would move from the snake outward into sea water, dehydrating the animal and killing it. On the other hand, if salt were to accumulate in the body until it was at the same concentration as sea water, the snake would die from excess salt, for unlike some marine organisms, it cannot tolerate such high concentrations.

There are various ways snakes conceivably could maintain their concentration of salt below that of sea water. One is to eject salt from the body when it accumulates in excess amounts. Another is to retard the entry of salt into the body. A combination of tactics could be employed. How, in fact, do sea snakes do it?

GETTING RID OF EXCESS SALT

One way to get rid of excess salt without losing a corresponding amount of water is to excrete very concentrated urine. Mammals commonly employ this method. For this to be effective in sea snakes, they would have to produce urine that was more concentrated in salts than the concentration of their body fluids — that is, to get rid of relatively more salt than water. When I first started studying marine snakes, I knew from the previous work of others that the kidneys of sea snakes (like those of land snakes) were not capable of concentrating salts at higher levels in the urine than in the blood. How, then, do sea snakes get rid of excess salt without losing precious water at the same time?

I reasoned that if the kidneys were a poor salt excretor, there must be a salt-secreting organ somewhere else in the body. It was already known that sea birds and some desert lizards had salt glands in their nasal passages. These produce concentrated brine that can be expelled by sneezing. Perhaps sea snakes had something similar.

In 1968 I set out to discover whether sea snakes could excrete salts by some means other than via the kidney. For this study, I used granulated file snakes (*Acrochordus granulatus*) that I collected from mangrove swamps in New Guinea and brought to my laboratory at the University of New England. The design of the experiment was simple. I first scrubbed the snakes in fresh water to remove any salt on the

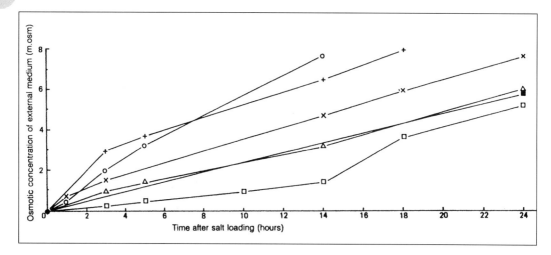

surface of the skin. Then I injected sterile salt brine into the body cavity of each snake so that it had excess salt to excrete. I placed the
snakes individually in glass jars of distilled, de-ionised water (pure
water without salts) and subsequently at intervals I took small samples of this water and measured the amount of salt, if any, being produced by the snakes.

To prevent contamination of the water by salts from the faeces or
urine, I sealed off the snakes' vents by fitting a contraceptive condom
over each snake's tail. This technique worked beautifully and kept all
faeces and urine sealed in. However, it did cause wonderment by the
chemist who sold the daily supply of condoms to my research assis-
tant, who casually explained I needed a receipt because the condoms
were for my research. Granting agencies also developed curiosity as to
why I was buying condoms from public funds.

The swimming of the snakes in the jars mixed the water so that
the samples accurately reflected the salt concentration. The water in
each jar soon had some salt in it and the concentration of salt progressively increased (Figure 7.1). Clearly, the snakes were secreting
salt into the water by some means other than via the kidney but where
was the source?

At that same time, Bill Dunson at Pennsylvania State University
was also interested in the sea snakes' salt problem and was working
on *Laticauda semifasciata* and *Pelamis platurus*. He found that high
concentrations of salt occurred in the mouth. He found a patch of
gland-like tissue in the front of the roof of the mouth and gave it the
name 'natrial gland' (salt gland) as he believed it to be the source of
the salt. Later, however, he found that such was not the case but
rather the salt emanated from a gland in the floor of the mouth under

Figure 7.1
The excretion of
salt by *Acrochordus
granulatus*. Each
curve represents
the history of a
different individual.
The snakes had
their cloacas sealed
off so the increase
in salt concentra-
tion in the water
around them was
by some means
other than via the
kidney. (From
Heatwole and
Taylor 1967)

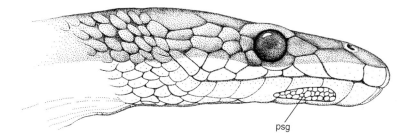

Figure 7.2
The sublingual salt gland of *Pelamis platurus*. The gland empties into the tongue-sheath and when the snake protrudes its tongue it expels the brine into the sea. psg = posterior sublingual salt gland (From Dunson 1979)

the tongue-sheath. This gland is a modified salivary gland called the sublingual gland. It empties salt brine into the canal of the tongue-sheath (Figure 7.2) and when the snake protrudes its tongue, it expels the brine into the sea. Further investigation showed that sea kraits, true sea snakes and *Acrochordus granulatus* all secrete salt via the sublingual gland. Thus, modification of this gland as a salt excretor has occurred independently at least twice in the evolution of these marine snakes, once in the lineage leading to *Acrochordus granulatus,* and once (and perhaps twice) in the one leading to sea kraits and true sea snakes.

By contrast, the homalopsines have solved the problem in a slightly different way. They have a salt gland, called the premaxillary gland located in the anterior end of the roof of the mouth. Natricine saltmarsh snakes do not have a salt gland.

Other marine reptiles show further variations on this theme. Sea turtles secrete salt from the eye as concentrated tears from the Harderian (tear) gland, saltwater crocodiles have small salt glands scattered over the tongue, and the marine iguana — a lizard that dives in the sea off the Galapagos Islands and eats marine algae — has a nasal salt gland reminiscent of those of sea birds and desert lizards.

PERMEABILITY OF THE SKIN TO SALT AND WATER

The skin of sea snakes is remarkably resistant to the passage of water. Most marine snakes tested (including *Acrochordus granulatus*, homalopsines, laticaudids and hydrophiids) allow water through the skin at rates less than half (3–47 per cent) that observed in freshwater snakes, and so loss of water to the sea via the skin is reduced. There are two species of *Hydrophis* that are exceptional in having somewhat higher permeabilities (up to 82 per cent that of freshwater snakes).

The saltmarsh and estuarine races of *Nerodia* have skin that is less permeable to salt and water than is that of the freshwater races of the same species. They also do not drink sea water whereas the latter do.

So it is a combination of behavioural traits and greater impermeability of the skin that allows these snakes to survive salty water, even without salt glands.

One of the interesting features of the permeability of sea snake skin is that it does not resist the passage of water equally in both directions. It permits water to move inward more rapidly than outward, an obvious advantage in the marine environment.

Relative impermeability of the skin of marine snakes to water would be of little significance if it freely allowed the passage of salt inwards. The body fluids, although retaining water, would be swamped with salt and the concentration would become too high. However, sea snake skin is resistant to the passage of salts inward and very little of the salt in the water in which the snakes are immersed succeeds in entering via the integument.

In summary, marine snakes can survive indefinitely in sea water partly because their skins are unusually resistant to the passage of water outward from the body and to the passage of salts inward. Water and salts are contained in the food and in the sea water that is drunk or accidentally ingested while swallowing a fish; most of the water from these sources is retained while excess salt is excreted by special salt glands (except in saltmarsh natricines).

DRINKING

Snakes with salt glands might be expected to drink sea water and excrete the excess salt, whereas those lacking salt glands would be expected to drink fresh water but reject sea water. The actual situation is more variable than that.

In captivity, the estuarine homalopsine *Cerberus rynchops* has been observed to drink fresh water and it is likely that it also would do so in nature.

Laticaudids that come out onto land to rest have periodic access to fresh water and indeed Michael Guinea has observed them drinking rain water from puddles and depressions in leaves and flicking the tongue against dew drops and raindrops. During rain, laticaudids were seen hanging nearly vertically from shrubs and drinking rain from leaves and from the runoff from their own bodies as it flowed downward to the head.

There would seem to be very little fresh water to drink in the sea. However, during heavy rain on an exceptionally calm sea, a surface layer of fresh water would float on the heavier sea water and would constitute a potential source of water for sea snakes. Hydrophiids need to be investigated in this respect.

The freshwater and estuarine races of natricines differ in their drinking behaviour. The freshwater races drink sea water and suffer accordingly, whereas the races from saline habitats do not drink sea water. This behavioural divergence may reflect physiological differences in that freshwater races may become thirstier because of a higher influx of sodium through their skin than occurs in the estuarine ones.

SALINITY PREFERENCES

Not all snakes inhabiting salty water prefer saline water to fresh water. Consequently habitat selection must result from responses to other environmental attributes that override salinity preferences.

David Zug and William Dunson gave a number of aquatic snakes a choice between saline and fresh water in aquaria. Fully hydrated *Cerberus rynchops*, a marine homalopsine, did not exhibit a preference for one kind of water over another. However, after severe dehydration this species showed a strong preference for fresh water. The sea krait *Laticauda colubrina*, despite being marine, actually preferred fresh water. Freshwater and estuarine races of natricines also preferred fresh water to full-strength sea water. At weaker saline solutions (15 per cent sea water or less) there was either no preference shown or a slight preference for the weakly saline water over fresh water.

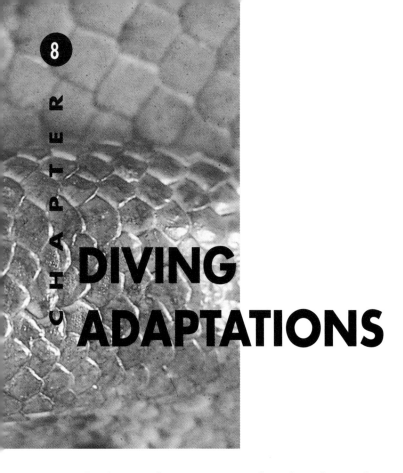

CHAPTER 8

DIVING ADAPTATIONS

The density of water is greater than that of air and provides a greater resistance to movement of animals through it. Methods of propulsion must be different in water than on land. How do sea snakes overcome the locomotory problems imposed by an aqueous medium? How do they regulate buoyancy in a liquid environment?

Most sea snakes spend much of their time submerged, often on the bottom at considerable depth. Under these circumstances how can such air-breathing animals obtain sufficent oxygen and get rid of carbon dioxide? Closely associated with the respiratory problem is one of hydrostatic pressure. An air-breathing animal whose air-filled lungs are subjected to intense hydrostatic pressure over a long time would suffer the bends (Caisson disease). How do sea snakes avoid the bends? Also at such pressures, how do they keep the air from being squeezed out of their lungs and lost?

MORPHOLOGICAL ADAPTATIONS

All snakes, even terrestrial ones, can swim and do so by lateral undulations of the body in much the same fashion as sea snakes. However, the flattened, paddle-shaped tail of all of the hydrophiids (Plates 11,

Figure 8.1
Acrochordids and
most hydrophiids,
such as the
Hydrophis elegans
pictured here, have
ventral scales the
same size as the
scales on the rest of
the body, or only
slightly enlarged.
(Photograph by the
author)

14) and laticaudids (Plate 7) almost certainly enhances the propulsive thrust, thereby making for more effective and rapid swimming.

Not all marine snakes have paddle-like tails. The natricines (Plate 5) and some of the homalopsines (Plates 1–4) have tails very similar to those of land snakes, whereas other homalopsines have tails that are slightly compressed. The acrochordids have a muscle that forms the skin of the tail and body into a small keel during swimming. The natricines, homalopsines and acrochordids usually occupy rather shallow or quiet water where they would not have to contend with wave action or such strong currents as do hydrophiids and laticaudids. There are exceptions, however, and both acrochordids and homalopsines sometimes occur in intertidal drainages where, although major wave action is not encountered, the snakes would be subject to currents.

Land snakes have large, transverse scales on the belly arranged in such a way that the rear edge overlaps the anterior end of the next scale behind so that forward movement of the belly along the ground is not impeded. However, backward movement results in the posterior, free edge of the scale catching against irregularities in the surface of the ground. These edges are used in gripping the substrate thereby aiding propulsion across the land surface. Such scales would have little effect in the sea and do not function in swimming. Accordingly, while homalopsines and laticaudids, both of which spend some time on land, and some hydrophiids such as *Aipysurus* (Plate 23), have retained rather large belly scales, the hydrophiids and acrochordids, which seldom, if ever, leave the water, have the ventral scales much reduced in size, in some cases nearly as small as the dorsal ones (Figure 8.1).

Even land snakes are not highly adapted to movement over loose, shifting substrates. Some desert species employ a looping movement of the body, called 'sidewinding' that appears to 'roll' the snake over loose sand and leaves characteristic tracks. It is interesting that *Laticauda colubrina* also sidewinds when having to cross loose, dry sand. When heading toward the sea from land, it engages in the usual form of serpentine terrestrial locomotion on firm substrates but when it encounters loose sand on the beach it sidewinds across it, returning to normal terrestrial locomotion again when firm, wet sand is encountered near the water's edge. The homalopsine *Bitia hydroides* forages

Figure 8.2
Nostril valves of
Aipysurus laevis in
the closed position
(left) and held open
by a needle
(right). Note that
the flap is attached
on the rear and
opens by folding
down into
the nostril.
(Photographs by
the author)

in muddy intertidal areas. It uses lateral undulatory movements in swimming through water and thin mud but sidewinds on the surface of somewhat firmer mud.

Valves that keep air in and sea water out are an important morphological adaptation of marine snakes. The scales of the mouth are close-fitting and when the mouth is closed it is sealed except for a small opening through which the tongue can be protruded. The anal scales extend backward, covering the cloaca, sealing it and protecting it against abrasion.

The most important valves, however, are those in the openings of the nostrils. In hydrophiids they are flaps that are attached on the rear border and bend inward when open (Figure 8.2). Closure of the flap seals out the water and keeps in the air. The operation of this valve is by erectile tissue, similar to that responsible for erection of the penis in mammals. When the spongy tissue becomes engorged with blood it swells and pushes the nostril flap upward, thereby closing it. Draining of the blood from the tissue allows the flap to droop and open.

The nostril closure of other aquatic snakes is less elaborate. In the laticaudids, acrochordids and homalopsines the erectile tissue surrounding the nasal passage swells and occludes the nostril.

DIVING CAPABILITY

There are a few air-breathing animals that have remarkable abilities to dive to great depths and remain submerged for extended periods. Among the most accomplished of these are whales, seals and penguins. To this list must be added the sea snakes. Some species that feed and rest on the bottom submerge to a depth of 100 metres. They can remain underwater for about two hours. Not all species have this maximum capability and even those that do, do not always exercise it. Fortunately for herpetologist-divers that want to study them firsthand, many species frequently are found in much shallower water.

I was intrigued by the outstanding diving ability of sea snakes. When I first began studying them, nothing was known about the physiological mechanisms that made such prowess possible, so I set

Plate 1
The homalopsine snake, *Bitia hydroides*, from near the mouth of the Muar River, Malaysia. (Photograph courtesy of Bruce Jayne)

Plate 2
The dog-faced snake or bockadam (*Cerberus rynchops*) swallowing a fish head-first. (Photograph courtesy of Bruce Jayne)

Plate 3
The white-bellied mangrove snake (*Fordonia leucobalia*). This species inhabits intertidal mangrove areas and associated tidal mudflats in estuaries and protected coastal waters from northern Australia to the Bay of Bengal. (Photograph courtesy of Harold Cogger)

Plate 4
Richardson's mangrove snake (*Myron richardsonii*). This species is found in the intertidal zone of mangrove forests lining creeks, estuaries and protected coastlines of northern Australia and New Guinea. (Photograph courtesy of Harold Cogger)

Plate 5
The Carolina water snake (*Nerodia sipedon williamengelsi*), an inhabitant of brackish marshes, saltmarshes, tidal creeks and canals, as well as freshwater impoundments on the Atlantic coast of North Carolina in the United States. (Photograph courtesy of Alvin Braswell)

Plate 6
The granulated file snake (*Acrochordus granulatus*). Notice its loose, granular skin and pointed tail. This species occurs in a variety of habitats, including fresh water, estuaries, mudflats, mangrove swamps and coral reefs. (Photograph courtesy of Harold Cogger)

Plate 7
The banded sea krait (*Laticauda colubrina*) swimming in shallow water in a mangrove swamp at Loloate Island, Papua New Guinea (upper) and resting on land on Efaté Island, Vanuatu (lower). This amphibious species hunts eels in the sea but comes out on land to rest and to lay eggs. It is widely distributed from India to Japan and New Caledonia. (Photographs by the author)

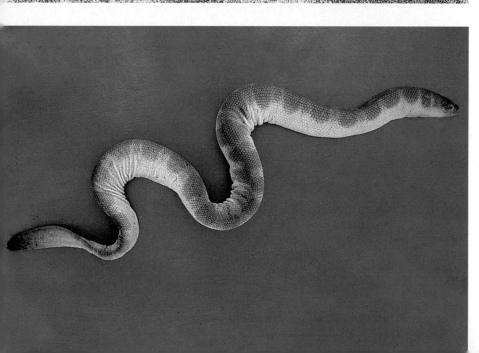

Plate 8

An olive sea snake (*Aipysurus laevis*) on a coral reef at Swain Reefs, Great Barrier Reef, Australia. This species is one of the most common species of sea snake on the Great Barrier Reef. It is restricted to coral reefs. It feeds on a wide variety of fish and even some invertebrates. (Photograph by the author)

Plate 9

The sea snake *Aipysurus apraefrontalis* has one of the most restricted distributions known. It is found only on a few small reefs on the north-western shelf of Australia. (Photograph courtesy of Harold Cogger)

Plate 11

Hardwick's sea snake (*Lapemis curtus*) from the Gulf of Carpentaria, Australia. This species is a common sea snake in various marine habitats from clear reefs to turbid estuaries. It is distributed from the Arabian Gulf to Asian and Australian waters. (Photograph by the author)

Plate 10
Three colour
patterns of the
turtle-headed
sea snake
(*Emydocephalus
annulatus*): slaty
grey (upper),
banded (centre)
and melanistic or
black (lower). The
slaty grey pattern
is widespread
throughout the
range of the species
from the Timor Sea
to the Great Barrier
Reef and the Coral
Sea. The banded
pattern is found at
some localities on
the Great Barrier
Reef and the
melanistic form is
characteristic of
populations at
Cato Island and
Saumarez Reef,
Australia. Note that
the snout of the
female is blunt
(upper) but that the
male has a sharp
spine on the tip of
his snout (lower;
not to be confused
with the tip of the
protruding tongue
just beneath it).
This species eats
only fish eggs; the
large, blade-like
scale of the
upper jaw is
used to scrape
eggs off corals.
(Upper and central
photographs cour-
tesy of Ron and
Valerie Taylor;
lower photograph
courtesy of Ben
Cropp)

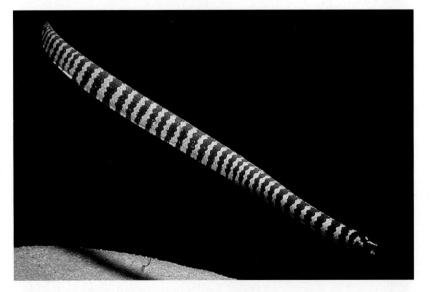

Plate 12
The beaked sea snake (*Enhydrina schistosa*) is usually found in shallow, muddy estuaries. It ranges from the Arabian Gulf to Australia and is responsible for about 90 per cent of human deaths from sea snake bite. (Photograph courtesy of Harold Cogger)

Plate 14
The yellow-bellied sea snake (*Pelamis platurus*), the most widely distributed species of snake in the world. This pelagic snake ranges from the waters of eastern Africa, along the Asian coasts to Japan, southward to the islands of the southwestern Pacific and across the Pacific Ocean to the western coast of the Americas. It is usually associated with slicks where it floats at the surface and attracts small fish to its shade, whereupon it attacks and eats them. Its colouration is probably a warning; it is seldom eaten by predators. (Photograph courtesy of Sherman Minton)

Plate 13
Two species of *Hydrophis* with different body forms: the elegant sea snake (*Hydrophis elegans*) from the Gulf of Carpentaria, Australia (upper) and a small-headed, long-necked species, the black-headed sea snake (*Hydrophis melanocephalus*) from Kura Island. (Upper photograph by the author; lower photograph courtesy of Harold Cogger)

Plate 15
Copulation of olive sea snakes (*Aipysurus laevis*). Below left: A mating pair on the Swain Reefs. Below right: A pair captured while they were copulating. The hemipenis of the male (brown snake) is inserted into the cloaca of the female (grey snake). (Left photograph courtesy of Glen Burns; right photograph by the author)

Plate 16
A female olive sea snake (*Aipysurus laevis*) fleeing and dragging a mating male (facing the camera) along by the hemipenis. (Photograph courtesy of Glen Burns)

Plate 17 (left)
A female olive sea snake (*Aipysurus laevis*) recaptured at Mystery Reef on 24 January 1984 that had been freeze-branded with the number 86 in July 1981. (Photograph by the author)

Plate 19 (right)
An olive sea snake (*Aipysurus laevis*) with its tongue extended, sensing its olfactory environment. Note that, unlike land snakes that pro-trude the entire tongue, sea snakes only protrude the forked tips of the tongue. (Photograph courtesy of Ben Cropp)

Plate 18
The author finding an ultrasonically tagged olive sea snake (*Aipysurus laevis*) using a Dukane underwater receiver. (Photograph courtesy of Rod Allin)

Plate 20
A horned sea snake (*Acalyptophis peronii*) with its head in a hole in the sand, searching for food. (Photograph courtesy of Ron and Valerie Taylor)

Plate 21
Skin shedding in the olive sea snake (*Aipyurus laevis*). Upper: A snake with oily secretions between the old and new skin making the eye appear cloudy. Lower: A snake crawling out of its skin, leaving the skin turned inside-out. (Photographs courtesy of Ron and Valerie Taylor)

Plate 22
An olive sea snake (*Aipysurus laevis*), with its skin heavily overgrown with algae. (Photograph courtesy of Ron and Valerie Taylor)

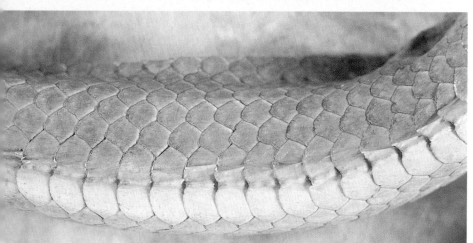

Plate 23
Some marine snakes, including homalopsines, laticaudids and some hydrophiids such as the olive sea snake (*Aipysurus laevis*) pictured here, have enlarged ventral scales, nearly as large as those of terrestrial snakes. (Photograph by the author)

Plate 24
The lung of an olive sea snake (*Aipysurus laevis*) showing the tracheal lung (T), the bronchial lung (B) and the saccular lung (S). Note the constriction between the saccular lung and the bronchial lung. (Photograph by the author)

Plate 25 (left)
Scanning electron micrograph of a fang of
Hydrophis curtus showing the aperture at the base
of the tooth where the venom duct enters the fang
and the exit hole at the tip. Note the dental groove
on the anterior face of the fang marking the
closure of the venom canal.
(From Gopalakrishnakone 1994)

Plate 26 (above)
The author holding a recently captured female
olive sea snake (*Aipysurus laevis*) while
Peter Saenger affixes a tag to its tail.
(Photograph provided by the author)

Plate 27
The author (left) and Dr Nobuo Tamiya (centre) examining a catch of *Laticauda semifasciata* at the sea snake fishery on Amami Oshima Island, Ryukyu Islands. (Photograph provided by the author)

Plate 28
The author milking the venom of an *Aipysurus duboisii* by placing a small plastic tube over an individual fang. (Photograph provided by the author)

Plate 29
Fang mark on the author's finger from a bite by an olive sea snake (*Aipysurus laevis*). (Photograph by Meg Lowman)

out to discover how they could dive so deeply and submerge so long. This investigation was to lead me into unexpected territory and to many surprises. On one hand, sea snakes were remarkably similar to land snakes but, on the other, they exhibited some unique features.

When surfacing to breathe, or descending back to the bottom, sea snakes move vertically in the water at about one metre every three seconds. At that rate, a snake at the maximum depth of 100 metres requires ten minutes just for the round trip to the surface for a breath! It is clearly an advantage for a deep-diving snake to remain submerged as long as possible so as to reduce the number of trips to the surface. Species inhabiting shallow water would have less of a time constraint upon them as trips to the surface could be made more quickly and not use up so much of the time they could otherwise devote to other activities.

I timed over 800 voluntary submergences of sea snakes from nine species and found they often stayed underwater for up to half an hour but that submergences of longer than an hour were less common. The longest submergence time I recorded was almost two hours. The time that a snake remains underwater depends in part on what it is doing. A sleeping or resting snake uses up less oxygen than an actively foraging one and consequently can remain submerged longer. How do sea snakes achieve such long times at the bottom? The following sections explore a variety of adaptations relating to diving capability.

METABOLISM

Energy is required to run the machinery of the body and food supplies that energy. In order for activity, growth, reproduction and other bodily functions to proceed that energy must be released and processed. All of the chemical reactions in the body that together carry out that function are collectively called metabolism.

The metabolic characteristics of reptiles differ greatly from those of birds and mammals. The latter groups regulate their body temperature at precise levels and maintain body heat by producing it themselves through a high rate of metabolism. Much of the oxygen used by a mammal or bird and much of the food energy it takes in goes into heat production. By contrast, reptiles produce very little metabolic heat and depend on outside sources for warmth. For example, land snakes may bask in the sun or seek out warm rocks from which they absorb heat. Sea snakes depend on water temperature and cannot maintain their body temperature above that of their surroundings. I measured the body temperatures of sea snakes underwater, immediately upon capture by inserting a quick-registering thermometer into the cloaca. The snakes always were at about the same temperature as that of the water around them (Figure 8.3). Even a darkly coloured snake resting at the surface and basking in the sun could only raise its temperature by less than 3°C because of rapid loss of heat to the water by conduction.

Because they do not maintain heat through metabolic means, the demand for oxygen and food by reptiles varies from about one-sixth to one-seventh that of a bird or mammal of the same size. That means that even terrestrial reptiles with no special diving adaptations should be able to hold their breaths six to seven times as long as terrestrial birds and mammals. If one takes two minutes as a maximum breath-hold capacity for a non-aquatic bird or mammal, then a reptile should be able to go without breathing for nearly 15 minutes. Indeed most land reptiles do not breathe regularly but intersperse breaths with variable, short periods of breath-holding (apnoea). It is clear, however, that the capacity of sea snakes for breath-holding is greater than that expected merely by the fact that they do not produce much metabolic heat.

Metabolism is of two kinds, aerobic and anaerobic. Aerobic metabolism involves the use of oxygen (O_2) for oxidising or 'burn-ing' the food fuels in order to lib-erate energy; carbon dioxide (CO_2) and heat are produced as by-products. We have already seen that mammals and birds engage in elevated rates of metab-olism as a means of producing heat for raising their body tem-perature. Aerobic metabolism (or aerobic respiration) can be mea-sured by the amount of oxygen used or by the amount of carbon dioxide produced. The first is the easiest and most common method.

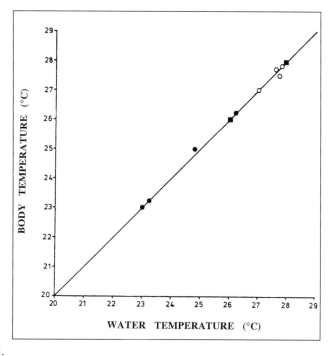

Figure 8.3 Relation of body temperature to water temperature at the site of capture of *Aipysurus laevis* (dots), *Aipysurus duboisii* (circles) and *Emydocephalus annulatus* (squares). The slanting line indicates body tem-perature and water temperature being equal. (From Heatwole 1981)

The second kind of metabolism, anaerobic metabolism (or anaer-obic respiration), is much less efficient in that it releases and process-es less energy but it does so by chemical pathways that do not involve oxygen immediately. However, by-products of anaerobic metabolism, such as lactic acid, are produced that are detrimental if they accu-mulate; eventually they must be oxidised. For this process oxygen is required and consequently the need for oxygen is not eliminated by anaerobic metabolism, merely delayed. The postponement of the need for oxygen during anaerobic respiration, when oxygen is not being used and lactic acid is being formed, can be thought of as building up an 'oxygen debt' which must be paid back when oxygen again becomes freely available. Then extra oxygen is used. Not only is the quantity for normal aerobic respiration required but also an additional amount for oxidising the accumulated lactic acid (paying back the oxygen debt).

For sea snakes, two theoretical strategies seemed possible and Roger Seymour and I set out to ascertain whether either of them applied. One was that snakes might prolong submergence time by building up an oxygen debt which they later repay while breathing at the surface. The second was that they might reduce their total energy use, and oxygen demands, by lowering their metabolic rate below that of land reptiles. Of course a combination of both could occur. What, in fact, does happen? Surprisingly, in most species neither does. Measurements of the change in oxygen content of the blood of snakes diving in the laboratory showed that they usually have enough oxygen to sustain aerobic metabolism, even after dives as long as, or longer than those normally occurring naturally in the sea. Also, lactic acid did not build up in the blood unless the animals were forced to remain under water for periods in excess of their normal submergence times. Furthermore, observations of the breathing of sea snakes in their natural habitat indicate that they usually take only one to three breaths quickly at the surface and dive again. These few breaths are insufficient to pay back an oxygen debt. Even in air, hydrophiids do not breathe in the same manner as land reptiles. Rather, they hold their breath for the same length of time that they do when submerged and only break those prolonged periods of apnoea by one or a few breaths.

Figure 8.4
The metabolic rate (as indicated by millilitres of oxygen used per gram of body weight per hour) of marine and terrestrial snakes. The line represents the average condition for land snakes. The circles represent values for different individuals of the yellow-bellied sea snake (*Pelamis platurus*). The dots represent means for various species of hydrophiid snakes. The star represents the mean for *Acrochordus granulatus*, a marine file snake.

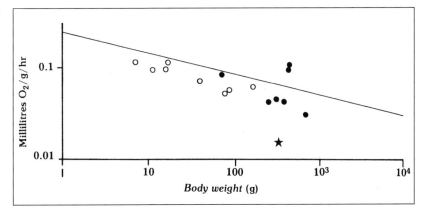

Clearly, sea snakes normally do not build up oxygen debts and do not employ anaerobic metabolism as a means of prolonging submergence time. Roger Seymour estimated that anaerobiosis in sea snakes would only occur in nature perhaps once in about every 100–200 dives. This is surprising as many land reptiles use anaerobic metabolism to sustain bursts of intense activity and some lizards do so when escaping predators by diving into streams.

Metabolic rate is dependent in part on the size of the animal, smaller ones using proportionately more oxygen for their weight than do larger ones. Consequently comparisons of metabolic rates of sea snakes and land snakes must take body size into consideration. When this is done, it is clear that sea snakes do not have consistently lower rates of oxygen consumption than do land snakes (Figure 8.4). Therefore, the reason marine snakes can remain submerged so long is not because of greatly lower metabolic rates than those of land snakes. There is one exception, the granulated file snake (*Acrochordus granulatus*). It has an extremely low metabolic rate that undoubtedly extends its submerged times (Figure 8.4).

Metabolic rate is dependent on body temperature. Land reptiles bask and in other ways behaviourally regulate their body temperature and in this way indirectly control their metabolic rate. Tropical to subtropical marine snakes live in an environment where the temperature does not change much during the day or even throughout the year compared to temperate localities. However, there are some temperature differences with depth and submergence time might be prolonged by the colder conditions of a deep dive.

OXYGEN STORAGE

Since most sea snakes do not use either anaerobic metabolism or depressed metabolic rates to increase time spent on the bottom, perhaps they are able to prolong submergence by taking down a large store of oxygen with them. There are several ways this could be achieved. They could have a larger lung capacity than land snakes and thus carry a greater supply of air with them. Another means would be to hold a greater amount of oxygen in the blood. These characteristics are examined in turn.

LUNGS

The lungs of snakes are unusual in comparison to those of other terrestrial vertebrates. Instead of being paired, they consist of a single hollow tube, divided into regions (Plate 24). The central section is the lung proper (termed the bronchial lung). It has a finely divided network of blood vessels in the wall and oxygen and carbon dioxide exchange takes place between the blood in the blood vessels and the air in the lung. The anterior section is called the tracheal lung and it is really the windpipe (trachea) which has become modified by an expansion of the dorsal part to the diameter of the bronchial lung and, unlike the windpipes of other vertebrates, has walls that are heavily suffused with blood vessels, just like real lung tissue. Its identity as the windpipe is only known because of the remnants of the supporting tracheal cartilages that remain embedded in the lower wall. The tracheal lung clearly functions in much the same way as the real lung and assists in the exchange of respiratory gases. In recognition of their similarity of function, the bronchial and tracheal lungs collectively are called the vascular lung. The posterior section, the saccular lung, is a blind pouch with so few blood vessels that it clearly cannot serve as a significant site for exchange of respiratory gases. It serves as an organ of air storage.

In this regard, the physics of lung shape should be discussed. When a round lung is stretched out into a thin tube, the ratio of surface area to volume changes. A nearly spherical lung has more space inside and can hold a greater volume of air than does a long tubular lung with the same surface area. The amount of surface area determines how fast oxygen and carbon dioxide can be exchanged: the larger the surface, the greater is the amount of gas that passes through it during a given time. However, the amount of oxygen available is determined by the volume of air. Since a tubular lung has relatively less air for the same surface area, it would be depleted sooner than would an equivalent, rounder lung. So the elongate body shape of snakes imposes a severe limitation on the amount of air available, even though the vascular lung provides quite an adequate respiratory surface. The extension of the lung rearwards, as the saccular lung, compensates by providing additional volume. This is useful in land snakes during prolonged swallowing when the air supply may be cut off by prey in the throat and in sea snakes during both swallowing and diving. Also during inhalation (breathing in) the stale air in the lung moves backward into the saccular lung, leaving the vascular surfaces of the other sections of lung in contact with fresh air, thereby increasing respiratory efficiency.

I was able to demonstrate experimentally that the saccular lung actually does prolong submergence time. When the saccular lung of the banded sea krait (*Laticauda colubrina*) was tied off surgically, submergence time decreased but was restored to its original duration when the passage between the saccular and bronchial lungs was reopened. The saccular lung also may function in buoyancy control (see page 94).

In view of the above discussion, it is clear that the features of sea snake lungs probably arose as an adaptation to lack of oxygen during swallowing of large prey but by good fortune could be put to use during diving. However, sea snakes have augmented other characteristics of land snake lungs that may have special significance in the marine environment. In land snakes the saccular lung is thin-walled and membraneous whereas in sea snakes it is thick-walled and contains muscles. The probable function of the more muscular saccular lung in sea snakes is the mixing of the air inside the lungs. As oxygen becomes depleted in the vascular lung below the level in the saccular lung, contraction of the muscles around the saccular lung would squeeze the storage air forward where its oxygen could be absorbed. This would be especially important for a resting snake without swimming movements to aid mixing of the air.

The acrochordids are an exception to the lung structure described above. They have a kind of lung unlike that of any other vertebrate. It is composed of a tube-within-a-tube. The inner tube has small holes in its lateral walls that communicate with the outer tube. The outer tube is partitioned into a series of self-contained compartments that communicate with each other only via the central tube. The functional significance of this unique arrangement is not known.

BLOOD

Increasing the amount of oxygen carried by the blood could be achieved either by (1) having more blood than land snakes of equivalent size, thereby providing a greater capacity for oxygen storage, or (2) having better blood, with a given amount of blood being able to hold more oxygen than is true of land snakes. The latter quality is measured by the blood oxygen capacity (the percentage of the volume of saturated blood made up of oxygen). Improved blood oxygen capacity could be achieved either by increasing the volume of blood cells per unit volume of blood (hematocrit) or by producing more effective haemoglobin.

The blood volumes of most reptiles, including aquatic and terrestrial ones, as well as different taxa (lizards, snakes, turtles, crocodilians), are mostly between 5 per cent and 6 per cent (Table 8.1). Although several species of sea snakes exceed the usual reptilian range with values greater than 9 per cent and the mean for the Hydrophiidae is slightly higher than for reptiles in general (6.8 per cent), some marine snakes have lower values. Indeed blood volumes falling well below the usual range for reptiles have been recorded from *Pelamis platurus* and *Cerberus rynchops*; each 3.9 per cent (Table 8.1). So marine snakes do not consistently have greater blood volumes

Table 8.1

Blood characteristics of equatic snakes compared to some terrestrial snakes

Family & Species	Hematocrit (%)	Blood Volume (%)	Oxygen Capacity (vol. %)	Habitat
ACROCHORDIDAE				
Acrochordus arafurae	21.6	—	—	Fresh water
Acrochordus granulatus	41.0, 50.1, 57.2	12.5, 13.3	16.2, 19.8	Fresh water and marine
Acrochordus javanicus	21.0	—	16.2	Fresh water
HOMALOPSINAE				
Cerberus rynchops	32.2	3.9	3.6	Marine, shallow
NATRICINAE				
Nerodia fasciata	22.0	—	—	Semi-aquatic, fresh and salty water
Nerodia sipedon	29.5	—	9.3	Semi-aquatic, fresh and salty water
LATICAUDIDAE				
Laticauda colubrina	24.3, 29.8, 34.9	5.9, 6.5	10.7, 10.9, 11.0	Amphibious marine
HYDROPHIIDAE				
Acalyptophis peronii	27.6, 32.7	5.0, 5.5, 5.9	7.9	Deep marine
Aipysurus apraefrontalis	28.3	—	—	Shallow marine
Aipysurus duboisii	35.8	5.7, 6.4	—	Marine
Aipysurus foliosquama	35.3	—	—	Shallow marine
Aipysurus laevis	32.8, 33.4	6.0, 7.5, 8.3	12.7	Marine
Astrotia stokesii	35.7	—	—	Marine
Emydocephalus annulatus	29.8, 31.3	5.0, 7.5, 7.9	6.5	Marine
Hydrophis coggeri	29.4, 30.9, 35.8	5.9, 9.1, 9.2, 9.9	10.8	Marine
Hydrophis cyanocinctus	32.2	—	—	Marine
Hydrophis elegans	33.7	—	—	Deep marine
Hydrophis semperi	38.2	—	—	Fresh water
Lapemis curtus	31.6	9.8	—	Marine
Pelamis platurus	26.5, 26.6	3.9	10.2	Marine, surface pelagic
ELAPIDAE				
Naja naja	24.0	—	—	Terrestrial
Pseudechis porpohyriacus	28.2	—	—	Semi-aquatic, fresh water
OTHER SNAKES				
Other semi-aquatic Natricinae	31.8 (4 spp.)	4.6 (1 sp.)	7.6 (1 sp.)	Semi-aquatic
Terrestrial Colubridae	29.1 (12 spp.)	5.8 (3 spp.)	6.6 (9 spp.)	Terrestrial
Boidae	27.0 (3 spp.)	—	8.2 (4 spp.)	Terrestrial
Viperidae	25.5 (7 spp.)	5.4 (1 sp.)	9.2 (2 spp.)	Terrestrial
Xenopeltidae	—	—	10.0 (1 sp.)	Terrestrial
TURTLES	27.6 (21 spp.)	6.0 (4 spp.)	7.8 (13 spp.)	Semi-aquatic to aquatic
CROCODILIANS	27.2 (5 spp.)	5.8 (1 sp.)	9.5 (3 spp.)	Semi-aquatic
LIZARDS	29.3 (24 spp.)	5.2 (4 sp.)	9.2 (38 spp.)	Terrestrial

Note: Values are means. Where multiple values are listed, they are from different literature sources.

than other reptiles and increased blood volume does not seem to have been a major route of adaptation to prolonged submergence.

There is one notable exception to this generalisation: *Acrochordus granulatus*. This species has a blood volume much higher than other snakes (average about 13 per cent) and so, everything else being equal, could carry a greater amount of oxygen in its blood during dives than could other species.

If a large blood capacity is not an important adaptation of most marine snakes, perhaps instead the blood they do have may have a higher concentration of red blood cells that would allow them to increase the amount of oxygen stored for diving. However, this does not seem to be the case, at least consistently. The average hematocrit of most reptiles falls between about 25 per cent to slightly over 30 per cent (Table 8.1). A number of species of hydrophiids and laticaudids lie toward the upper end of this range or exceed it by several per cent. While on average their blood is slightly richer than that of many other reptiles, the differences are not impressive and alone would not seem to constitute a major adaptation. Again the sole outstanding exception is *Acrochordus granulatus*. It has an hematocrit of about 50 per cent, double that of some snakes and the highest known for any vertebrate.

The blood oxygen capacities of most sea snakes are little different from those of land snakes or other reptiles. Most reptiles have values in the range of 6.5–10.0 volume per cent. Values for most marine snakes either lie within the upper part of that range or exceed it by a few per cent (Table 8.1); on the other hand, some species are at the lower end of the range (*Emydocephalus annulatus*) or fall well below it (*Cerberus rynchops*). As in so many other attributes, *Acrochordus* is exceptional. Its blood oxygen capacity is more than double that of some other species and the highest one reported for reptiles, perhaps not surprising when it is remembered that it also has a high hematocrit.

Another feature of the blood of sea snakes may be relevant to diving. As carbon dioxide builds up, as it does during breath-holding, it causes the blood to release more oxygen than it would otherwise. This effect of carbon dioxide on oxygen release is called the Bohr shift. The greater the Bohr shift, the greater is the amount of oxygen that can be delivered. It might be expected that sea snakes would have a greater Bohr shift than land snakes and in this way make better use of the oxygen carried by their blood and prolong their stay underwater. However, this does not seem to be the case. Roger Seymour found that there is variability in the extent of the Bohr shift among species of snakes but it does not correlate with the type of environments they occupy. Rather, it seems to be related to activity levels. Active species with high metabolic rates have a large Bohr shift and sluggish species with low metabolic rates have a small one.

Several unusual species deserve special comparison. The granulated file snake (*Acrochordus granulatus*) shows a number of adaptations that are either lacking or relatively inconspicuous in a number of other marine snakes. Not only can it store large amounts of oxygen for dives by virtue of its great blood volume, high hematocrit and large oxygen capacity, it can also use oxygen very slowly because of its low metabolic rate (see page 78, Metabolism). In contrast, the bockadam (*Cerberus rynchops*), despite having a rather high hematocrit, has an unusually low blood volume and oxygen capacity. This species inhabits shallow water and often can breathe merely by lifting its head out of the water. It is curious, however, that it has lower blood volume and oxygen capacity than even many terrestrial reptiles.

Laticauda colubrina, while not outstanding in any of the blood properties mentioned above, is more versatile than other marine snakes in one regard. The temperature of the sea does not vary so greatly as it does in the terrestrial environment and most marine snakes do not make adjustments in their blood oxygen capacities in response to changing temperature. Harvey Pough and Harvey Lillywhite found that *Laticauda colubrina*, which comes out on land and thus is subjected to a greater range of temperature variation than are the hydrophiids, resembles land snakes in its capacity to adjust blood oxygen capacity in response to fluctuating temperatures.

In conclusion, it seems that most marine snakes do not have any special or unusual attributes of the blood that help explain their ability to endure long submergences. Except for *Acrochordus granulatus*, they do not consistently have either more blood or better blood than land snakes, and the extent of the Bohr shift seems related to activity level rather than to a marine way of life. *Laticauda colubrina* resembles land snakes more than other marine snakes in its ability to adjust its blood oxygen capacity to changing temperatures.

In any event, factors other than availability of oxygen may limit the length of time snakes dive. Roger Seymour and the late Max Webster found that hydrophiids often use only about one half of their oxygen reserves between breaths.

RESPIRATION THROUGH THE SKIN

Membranes that are involved in respiratory exchange of oxygen and carbon dioxide are usually thin and richly supplied with small blood vessels. Consequently the heavy, scaly skin of sea snakes would not seem to be a likely site for respiratory activity. That was the line my reasoning took when Roger Seymour and I contemplated the problem of the prolonged diving of sea snakes. However, science deals with facts and observations as the basis for understanding, not with reasoning alone. Often as one of the steps in discovering the real answer to a problem, one must eliminate other possible explanations. That was my motive for attempting to measure the passage of oxygen through the skin of sea snakes.

I knew that some day after a seminar on my research, one of those persons, present in every audience, who spend the entire hour trying to ferret out the most embarrassing question they could possibly ask the speaker, would enquire, 'How do you know that sea snakes can't dive for such long times because they respire through the skin, like frogs? Have you tested this?' It would be inadequate merely to point out the unlikelihood that appreciable quantities of respiratory gases would pass through a thick, scaly skin. One would need data to indicate that tests had been made and to show that the amount of oxygen entering the snake's body via the skin was negligible.

Table 8.2

Proportion of oxygen uptake that occurs through the skin in marine snakes and a terrestrial snake

Family & Species	Mean Cutaneous Oxygen Uptake (% of total respiration)
HYDROPHIIDAE	
Acalyptophis peronii	10.8
Aipysurus duboisii	10.8
Aipysurus laevis	21.6
Hydrophis coggeri	0*
Lapemis curtus	5.2
Pelamis platurus	21.7
ACROCHORDIDAE	
Acrochordus granulatus	13.3
TERRESTRIAL SNAKE	
Constrictor constrictor 2.6	

* In other experiments this species took up oxygen through the skin at rates comparable to those of other hydrophiids.

We designed the following experiment. A snake was placed in a tube which was then filled to the brim with sea water and sealed so that no bubbles of air remained. The oxygen content of the water was measured initially and again after the snake had been in the container for 5–10 minutes. To our surprise, the amount of dissolved oxygen in the water had decreased whereas it had not done so in a tube containing sea water but no snake. Reluctant to accept our results, we thought perhaps micro-organisms on the skin of the snake might have consumed the oxygen. We repeated the exercise after washing the snake's skin with disinfectant but got the same result. Further experimentation by ourselves and others on a variety of species revealed that sea snakes really can take up oxygen through their skin, in some cases enough to supply one-fifth of their total needs (Table 8.2). Carbon dioxide is more soluble and most of that produced by sea snakes can be eliminated via the skin. Indeed respiration through the skin (cutaneous respiration) is one of the major adaptations of sea snakes to the marine environment.

Table 8.3
Absolute values of oxygen uptake through the skin in marine snakes and a terrestrial snake

Family & Species	Cutaneous Oxygen Uptake $(mLO_2/100g\ body\ wt/hr)$
LATICAUDIDAE	
*Laticauda colubrina**	0.7
*Laticauda laticaudata**	0.7
HYDROPHIIDAE	
Acalyptophis peronii	0.5
Aipysurus duboisii	0.5
Aipysurus laevis	0.7
Hydrophis coggeri	1.7
Hydrophis cyanocinctus	1.5
Hydrophis inornatus	1.9
Hydrophis ornatus	1.6
Lapemis curtus	0.5
Pelamis platurus	1.6
ACROCHORDIDAE	
Acrochordus granulatus (marine)	0.2
Acrochordus granulatus (freshwater)	0.7
HOMALOPSINAE	
Cerberus rynchops	0.5
TERRESTRIAL SNAKE.	
Constrictor constrictor 0.06	

* Snakes were active; all other values were obtained on inactive snakes.

Comparison of the respiratory capacity of the skin of different species of snakes revealed large differences. Land snakes have a very limited capacity for cutaneous respiration and can only absorb oxygen at about one-tenth to one-thirtieth the rate that marine snakes do (Table 8.3). Even among marine species the capacity for cutaneous respiration varies. *Hydrophis* and *Pelamis* take up three to four times more oxygen through the skin than do other genera of hydrophiids or than do the laticaudids, acrochordids and homalopsines.

Cerberus rynchops inhabits mangrove swamps and it exchanges relatively small amounts of oxygen through the skin (Table 8.3). The water of mangrove swamps is often low in oxygen because of high temperatures and because of the large amounts of stagnant organic mud. Conversely, levels of carbon dioxide often are high because of decaying organic matter. Uptake through the skin is dependent upon the difference in level of concentration of the gas in the water compared to the level in the blood, that is, the steepness of the gradient. Consequently, in the mangrove habitat a high permeability of the skin to these gases might be a disadvantage rather than an advantage.

The acrochordids inhabit very shallow water and would be able to surface easily for air. The laticaudids are not exceptionally deep divers and they spend considerable time on land where cutaneous respiration would not be essential.

There is a link beween the permeability of the skin to gases and to salt and water (see Chapter 7). Snake skins that permit easy passage of gases also tend to allow salt to pass. So there needs to be a balance between the role of the skin in regulating salt and water and its function in exchanging respiratory gases. The permeability of the skin may be a compromise between these conflicting needs.

THE DIVING SYNDROME

The heart pumps blood to the lungs and skin where oxygen is picked up and carbon dioxide eliminated. The blood then transports the oxygen to the tissues and releases it there, at the same time collecting carbon dioxide for movement back to lungs and skin. The role of the circulatory system in gathering, transporting and releasing respiratory gases means that it can have an important influence on diving capability. The properties of the blood have been discussed already (see page 80, Oxygen Storage) and in this section other aspects of the circulation are examined.

In most vertebrate air-breathing divers a number of coordinated events take place that together can be designated as the diving syndrome. When an animal dives, its immediate use of oxygen is reduced by starving the less vital organs of oxygen. This is achieved by constricting the blood vessels leading to those organs, thereby making the vessels smaller and reducing blood flow through them. The organs that are cut off from oxygen then undergo anaerobic respiration and accumulate lactic acid during the dive (see page 76, Metabolism).

The heart and brain are not capable of anaerobic respiration in most vertebrates and these organs must maintain an adequate supply of oxygen-rich blood. Accordingly, a smaller circuit of blood flow is maintained to these vital organs and to the lungs from which the supply of oxygen is obtained. The blood circulates from the heart to the lung, back to the heart, then to the brain and again back to the heart. Since most of the circulation to the body is cut off and only a reduced circuit is left in operation, the heart does not need to work so hard and it slows down. As a result, it does not require as much energy or use as much oxygen. The lowering of heart rate during diving is called diving bradycardia. It is characterised by a unique feature: it is insensitive to activity. Usually when an animal is very active, its heartbeat speeds up in accordance with the greater demand of its highly metabolising tissues for oxygen. This does not happen during diving bradycardia; the heart rate remains low regardless of how active the animal is.

Upon return to the surface where a renewed air supply is available, the animal breathes, expands the diameter of its blood vessels (vasodilation), increases its heart rate to normal level, re-establishes blood flow to all parts of the body and flushes out the accumulated lactic acid for oxidising by the now freely available oxygen. That is, it pays back its oxygen debt.

Although the diving syndrome is common to most vertebrate air-breathing divers, including some reptiles, it does not fit the data from marine snakes. First of all it has already been noted that sea snakes do not normally undergo anaerobic respiration or produce large amounts of lactic acid during dives, nor do they usually stay at the surface long enough, or breathe often enough, to pay back an oxygen debt. Second, the fact that they employ cutaneous respiration suggests that the diving syndrome is not applicable to them. Constricting blood flow to the peripheral part of the body would also cut off blood flow to the skin and make cutaneous respiration ineffective.

Yet sea snakes do exhibit certain responses to diving that are similar to parts of the diving syndrome. When they submerge the heart slows down and there is at least a superficial resemblance to diving bradycardia (Figure 8.5). Can this response be reconciled with the other data?

There is an important difference between the lower heart rate during diving in sea snakes and that in true diving bradycardia. Heart rate of diving sea snakes is dependent upon activity (Figure 8.5).

Unlike vertebrates with the diving syndrome, when an inactive, submerged sea snake becomes active, its heart rate increases and when it becomes inactive again, it decreases. A second feature is that change in heart rate seems to be related more to surfacing than to submergence. Precise measurement of the heartbeat of an inactive snake floating on the surface of the water (heart rate therefore not elevated by activity) shows that a few seconds before it takes a breath the heart rate speeds up but then drops again as soon as the animal has breathed. It seems that the snake has a quickened pulse, slightly in anticipation of breathing, and that at the time fresh air is being drawn into the lungs, blood is flowing through the respiratory surface at a rapid pace, thereby facilitating absorption of oxygen by the blood. So the change in heart rate in sea snakes is a quickening of the heartbeat during breathing (breathing tachycardia) rather than a slowing of heartbeat during diving. Put another way, the low rate of heartbeat of a sea snake is its 'normal' heart rate and it increases it above normal during breathing. In animals with the diving syndrome, the normal one is the higher heart rate at the surface and the departure from normal is the lowered one during diving bradycardia. This is not just a difference in definition of terms. It denotes a different function altogether. Diving bradycardia is part of a syndrome involving anaerobic respiration, oxygen debts, vasoconstriction and a reduced circuit of blood flow, whereas breathing tachycardia of sea snakes involves none of these but rather cutaneous respiration, aerobic metabolism underwater and enhanced exchange of oxygen across the lung during breathing. The only thing in common between these two phenomena is that heart rate changes between surfacing and diving.

Clearly use of cutaneous respiration has freed sea snakes from a number of restrictions imposed by submergence and they have adapted to the marine environment in quite different ways from diving mammals and birds. Some other reptiles, especially those that use diving merely to escape predators, seem to have the classical diving syndrome. Still others, especially freshwater turtles, may resemble sea snakes.

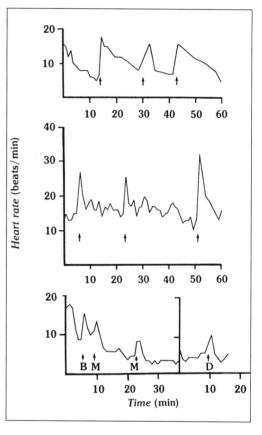

Figure 8.5
Heart rates of an hydrophiid, *Lapemis curtus* (top), a laticaudid, *Laticauda colubrina* (centre) and an acrochordid, *Acrochordus granulatus* (bottom). Top and centre: arrows = when a breath was taken. Bottom: B = a breath, M = a voluntary movement, D = a movement in response to prodding.

ALTERING CIRCULATION TO THE SKIN AND LUNGS

Figure 8.6
Structure of the heart of a mammal (upper: ventral view) and of a snake (lower: two dorsal views) one in contraction of the atria with filling of the ventricle (centre) and one with contraction of the ventricle and filling of the atria (bottom).
CA = cavum arteriosum; CP = cavum pulmonale;
CV = cavum venosum;
LA = left atrium;
LS = left systemic arch; PA = pulmonary artery;
RA = right atrium;
RS = right systemic arch; V = ventricle.
In the mammal all flows are indicated by black arrows; in the reptile white arrows indicate flow of oxygenated blood and black arrows indicate flow of stale blood.
(Diagram of mammalian heart (modified) by permission from W.W. Norton & Company Inc. Reptilian heart modified from Webb, Heatwole and de Bavay 1971)

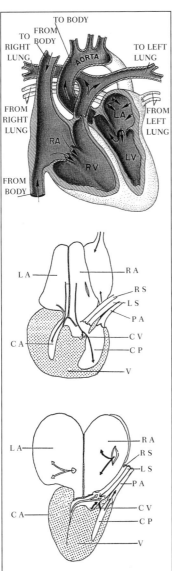

The hearts of mammals and birds have four completely separate chambers, two ventricles and two atria (Figure 8.6). The oxygen-rich blood from the lungs drains into one of these compartments (the left atrium) and is the only blood entering that cavity. From there, the blood flows through valves into the left ventricle. When the ventricle beats this blood is forced out of the heart through a large systemic vessel (aorta) that branches and carries oxygenated blood to the various parts of the body. While passing through the small blood vessels (capillaries) that service the body, this blood becomes depleted of its oxygen and is loaded with waste carbon dioxide, which it carries back to the heart, this time entering the right atrium, rather than the left one; it passes from there into the right ventricle. The right ventricle leads only into the pulmonary vessel that carries the stale blood to the respiratory surfaces of the lungs. There carbon dioxide is given off and oxygen taken up and the cycle starts over again. So there are two completely separate circulations of blood simultaneously passing through the heart: one with fresh blood coming from the lungs and going to the body and the other of stale blood coming from the body and going to the lungs. Because the chambers of the heart are completely separated, these two circulations do not mix.

The hearts of snakes are more complex and much more versatile than those of mammals or birds. There are three compartments, two atria and only one ventricle. The ventricle contains three partly interconnecting cavities (Figure 8.6). Another peculiar reptilian feature is that there are three, rather than two, major vessels exiting from the ventricle. There are two systemic vessels that carry blood to the body and one pulmonary one that carries blood to the lungs. This unique cardiac structure has a profound effect on the versatility of how snakes' hearts function, including adaptations related to diving.

The pattern of blood flow through the heart is affected by the shape and location of valves and partial partitions (septa) located in the ventricle and by the locations of the exits from the ventricle into the three major vessels. Freshly oxygenated blood from the lungs enters the left atrium, as in mammals, and from there passes through a valve into the ventricle. During contraction of the left atrium, blood pressure forces the flaps of the valve downward against one of the septa of the ventricle and deflects most of the blood into a deep cavity called the cavum arteriosum (Figure 8.6). The stale blood from the body drains into the right atrium and from there into a shallow cavity, the cavum venosum, and from there via an open flap in one of the ventricular septa into a deep cavity just below, the cavum pulmonale. Sometimes some blood is left behind in the cavum venosum. The cavum venosum lies between the cavum arteriosum and the cavum pulmonale, and under certain circumstances can be the site of varying degrees of mixing of the fresh and stale circulations. When the ventricle contracts during heart beat, the oxygenated blood in the cavum arteriosum pushes upward against the valves at the entrance of the atria and closes them, preventing blood from re-entering the atria. Instead, the blood is deflected towards the mouth of the systemic arteries. In this way, the fresh blood mainly goes to the body. By contrast, ventricular contraction forces the blood in the cavum pulmonale into the pulmonary artery located at its upper end, often closing the flap between the cavum pulmonale and cavum venosum. In this way, all or most of the stale blood goes to the lungs for replenishment of oxygen and elimination of carbon dioxide. So far, the pattern of blood flow does not seem very different from the circulation through the hearts of mammals and birds: fresh blood goes from the lungs to the body through the heart, while stale blood goes from the body to the lungs via a separate route through the heart. Indeed under some circumstances there is very little difference in the way the two kinds of heart function but the reptilian heart is more versatile by virtue of the incompletely divided ventricle. The stale and fresh circulations can be kept separate, but unlike mammals and birds, reptiles can also mix the two and alter the composition and amount of blood going to either the lungs or body. The openings of the two systemic vessels that lead from the heart to the body are located near the top of the cavum venosum and receive most of the blood expelled from that cavity during contraction of the ventricle. Slight changes in relative pressures among chambers and resistances to flow through the body or lungs can lead to a greater or lesser mixing of stale and fresh bloods, particularly in the cavum venosum, and to alteration in the relative flows through the systemic versus the pulmonary vessels. These changes in routing of blood within the heart are called cardiac shunts, with a left-to-right shunt sending more blood to the lungs relative to the body, and a right-to-left shunt being the reverse.

Cardiac shunts have a variety of functions in reptiles. For example, if transport of heat by the blood is temporarily of greater importance than transport of oxygen (as when a cold terrestrial snake with low metabolic rate is basking and picking up heat from the sun at the surface of the skin and needs to move that heat around the body), the blood can be mixed and more of it sent to the skin to pick up heat, with the lungs being bypassed by much of the flow. If transport of oxygen is of prime importance, as in a highly active snake, mixing of stale and fresh bloods can be abolished and more blood sent to the lungs for exchange of respiratory gases.

The significance of cardiac shunts in diving snakes is that the amount and quality of blood passing through the respiratory surfaces of lungs and skin can be regulated. For example, sending more blood to the body and less to the lungs would mean that the skin would be emphasised as a respiratory organ and oxygen in the lung would be husbanded. Sending a greater amount of blood through the lungs, rather than to the body, during breathing would enhance exchange of oxygen and carbon dioxide across the lung surface at that time. So sea snakes have a means of fine-tuning their circulatory pattern to meet their immediate respiratory needs. In addition, shunts may be involved in prevention of the bends (see page 92).

There are other ways of altering the flow of blood to the lungs. Some snakes have a blood vessel that directly connects the artery entering the lung with the vein leaving it. When that vessel is open most of the blood flows though it and does not go through the respiratory capillaries of the lung. However, when a muscle constricts and closes off that vessel, the blood cannot bypass the lung and pulmonary respiration takes place. This re-routing of the blood is called a pulmonary shunt.

Another peculiarity of the circulatory system of marine snakes is that the heart is located further from the head toward mid-body than it is in terrestrial or arboreal ones. A more centrally located heart may be an advantage in an aquatic snake because it equalises the flows and blood pressures between the two ends of the body. Terrestrial or arboreal snakes need to maintain blood pressure in the head when in a vertical position and they have various adaptations that achieve that, one of which is an anteriorly located heart. Aquatic snakes are supported externally by water pressure that nearly matches their blood pressure and are thus less affected by gravity when head-up. A more centrally placed heart and lack of special adaptations that prevent drops of blood pressure in the head have come about independently in at least three (possibly four) lineages: the homalopsines, the acrochordids and the hydrophiid/laticaudids.

THE BENDS

When an air-breather dives deeply, the air in its lungs is compresssed by pressure of the water. Such hydrostatic pressure forces more gas into solution in the blood than would occur at the pressures existing at the surface. In this way, hydrostatic pressure assists in the uptake of oxygen into the blood from air in the lung. However, air is about four-fifths nitrogen and nitrogen is forced into solution in the bloodstream as well. Unlike oxygen, nitrogen is not used by the animal and merely accumulates. Consequently after a deep, prolonged dive, the blood contains high levels of dissolved nitrogen. When the animal surfaces and the pressure is released, the nitrogen comes out of solution and forms bubbles in the bloodstream that can cause severe distress, crippling, or even death. This malady is called the 'bends' or Caisson disease.

Because sea snakes dive to great depths and remain submerged for extended periods, one would expect them to suffer the bends when they surface to breathe. How do they avoid this problem?

One school of thought is that they have no special adaptations and that they *are* subject to the bends. Proponents of this view point to a high mortality among sea snakes captured and kept on the surface. They believe that snakes normally avoid symptoms of the bends by remaining on the surface only long enough to catch a quick breath and submerge again before there is time for nitrogen bubbles to form. At depth whatever bubbles were beginning to form would be driven back into solution. However, many captured sea snakes that are kept at the surface show no ill effects and on calm days snakes in nature sometimes loll at the surface for extended periods and yet do not suffer the bends. This theory does not seem wholly adequate. There are other considerations.

One is that the rate of nitrogen absorption in the blood is regulated by the circulatory system (see pages 89–91). If blood flow were to be directed preferentially to the body and the lung bypassed, the

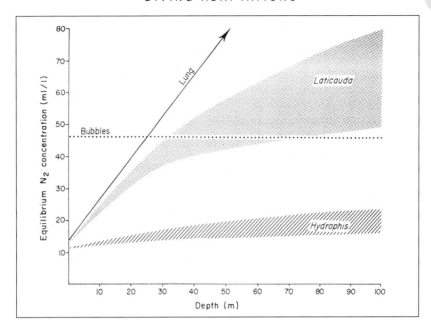

Figure 8.7
Concentrations of nitrogen in the lung (slanted line) and in the blood of the body of *Laticauda colubrina* (stippled) and of *Hydrophis coggeri* (hatched) at different depths. The dotted line indicates the nitrogen concentration at which one would expect bubbles of nitrogen to form in the blood when decompressing. (From Seymour 1982)

amount of gas, including nitrogen, taken up from the lung could be reduced. By regulating the flow of blood through the lungs, a balance might be achieved that would meet respiratory requirements and at the same time avoid the bends. This possibility suggests another way cutaneous respiration may be adaptive. The skin and body are on the same circulatory pathway and thus blood shunted to the body can still be oxygenated by cutaneous respiration. Exchange of respiratory gases through the skin, by supplementing the oxygen supply, might make it feasible to reduce blood flow through the lungs, thereby avoiding the bends.

A second consideration is that the excess nitrogen dissolved in the blood may merely pass into the sea through the skin. The skin is permeable to gases such as oxygen and carbon dioxide (see pages 84, 85), and consequently would probably also be permeable to nitrogen. However, to lose nitrogen through the skin it must be at a higher level in the blood than in sea water, a condition that would occur in snakes after prolonged submergence.

Roger Seymour estimated that the deep-diving *Hydrophis coggeri* (at the time referred to as *H. belcheri*) has such a large cardiac shunt and sufficiently high permeability of its skin to gases that its blood nitrogen would not rise to levels that would produce bubbles even after a dive to 100 metres. By contrast, *Laticauda colubrina*, a shallower diver, has lower skin permeability and a less pronounced cardiac shunt that would put it in danger at depths below 30–70 metres (Figure 8.7).

BUOYANCY CONTROL

A diving animal that is too buoyant will have to exert considerable energy, not only to get to the bottom, but to stay there. On the other hand, one that is heavier than water will have no trouble diving but will have to expend a greater amount of energy swimming to the surface. Some reptiles, crocodiles for example, adjust the amount of air they take in during the last breath before diving so that they are negatively buoyant (heavier than water) and tend to sink. When they are at the surface they breathe in a greater volume of air and can remain afloat effortlessly. They can adjust their buoyancy to meet immediate needs or to compensate for changes in their body weight after eating, or for changes in density of the water in which they are diving (salty water is denser than fresh water).

Pelamis platurus dives with enough air still in its lung to keep itself positively buoyant (lighter than water). However, as it moves deeper, the hydrostatic pressure compresses the air in its lung and the overall density of the animal increases accordingly; the snake becomes negatively buoyant as long as it stays at depth. As it subsequently uses up oxygen from the lung and passes carbon dioxide (and perhaps nitrogen) out through its skin, its specific gravity increases even more and it becomes negatively buoyant even under surface pressures. So during its initial dive it has to work against its tendency to float. Later, when surfacing, it has to counteract its tendency to sink. *Pelamis platurus* is primarily a surface-dwelling species and dives mainly to avoid choppy surface water or other unpleasant conditions. The buoyancy of bottom-dwelling species needs to be investigated, especially that of the turtle-headed sea snake (*Emydocephalus annulatus*) that accidentally ingests sand with its meal of fish eggs and consequently often must be rather heavy.

Control of body position may be influenced by the distribution of air within the lung. The bronchial lung is larger than either the tracheal or saccular one, and a horizontal snake may have its greatest lift at the centre of its body. However, the lung is a straight tube and is not compartmented (except in *Acrochordus*; see page 80, Oxygen Storage), so when the snake tilts upward toward the surface, the air in the lung would tend to rise towards the head and increase the buoyancy of the anterior end. The reverse would be true during diving and the tail end would be more buoyant. So such shifts of air within the lung may aid in maintaining a head-up position during ascent to the surface and a tail-up orientation when diving. The muscles of the saccular lung may assist in regulating the distribution of air within the lung and thereby affect the relative buoyancy of different parts of the body.

VENOM

Venom has multiple purposes: subduing and killing prey, assisting in digestion and defending against enemies. This chapter describes the kinds and composition of venom, tells how it is delivered and portrays the role it plays in the life of the snake.

THE VENOM APPARATUS

The venom apparatus of laticaudids and hydrophiids consists of the venom gland that secretes the venom, a fang that serves to inject it into the victim and a duct through which the venom passes between gland and fang (Figure 9.1). There is also accessory glandular tissue that secretes into the duct. In some land snakes this tissue occurs as a discrete gland near the point where the duct enters the fang but in others it encases the duct throughout its length. In sea snakes there is no sharp demarcation between the venom gland and the accessory gland. Rather there is a gradual transition from one to the other, the posterior part of the gland secreting mainly proteins and polypeptides (toxins) and the anterior, or accessory part, secreting mostly polysaccharides (mucus).

The venom glands of sea snakes are elongated, modified salivary glands that lie beneath the skin along the upper jaw on each side of the head (Figure 9.1). The venom is secreted into a central cavity or lumen. The glands are encased by a fibrous capsule attached to the adductor externus superficialis muscle, contraction of which expels the venom through the duct and fang into the victim.

Electron microscopic examination of venom has shown that it contains exceedingly minute globules. These globules are of several kinds and it may be that each kind contains a different component of the venom. It is not clear how the active components are released at an appropriate time to affect the prey. Perhaps this is one of the functions of the accessory part of the gland. In addition to secreting mucus as a lubricant, it may also add some chemical that releases the active components of the venom from their globules. It has been observed that there are fewer globules in venom having left the fang than in venom still in the gland. However, this could merely represent dilution by mucus.

Another possibility is that the globules react with some chemical in the victim's body that causes them to disintegrate and release the active components of the venom. Immunity of some species (such as the snakes themselves) to venoms may arise from absence of such an agent. All of this discussion is speculative and much work is required before the mechanism of envenomation is completely understood.

Part of the process of activation of toxins may be changes in the toxin molecules themselves. Some toxins, at least, are initially synthesised as a precursor consisting of two protein fragments. The shorter of these, called the leader sequence, facilitates the crossing of the toxin chain through cell membranes. Later the leader sequence is split and the molecule folds into a complex form and acquires its toxic properties. What causes such folding is poorly understood.

The fangs of laticaudids and hydrophiids are located,

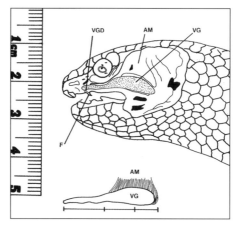

Figure 9.1
Head of an olive sea snake (*Aipysurus laevis*). Above: showing the fang, and with the skin of the lateral part of the head removed to show the venom gland and its associated duct and muscles. Below: a diagram of that head indicating the location of the adductor externus superficialis muscle (AM), fang (F), venom gland (VG) and duct of the venom gland (VGD). The diagram shows the attachment of the adductor muscle to the venom gland. (Photograph and diagram courtesy of Shantay Zimmerman)

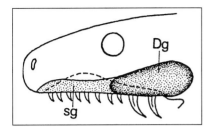

Figure 9.2
Diagram of the skull of a rear-fanged colubrid snake showing Duvernoy's gland and its association with enlarged, grooved rear teeth. Dg = Duvernoy's gland, sg = superior labial gland. (Diagram with permission from *The Life of Reptiles,* volume 1, by Angus Bellairs, Weidenfeld and Nicholson.)

one on each side, in the front of the mouth at the anterior end of the maxillary bone. Unlike the vipers, which have a complicated mechanism that swings their long fangs upward toward the roof of the palate when the mouth is closed and erects them when the mouth is open, venomous marine snakes (like their relatives, the elapids) have relatively short, fixed fangs that rotate only sightly during biting.

Stokes' sea snake (*Astrotia stokesii*) has a deeply grooved fang with the edges of the groove not closing to form a central canal. In other venomous sea snakes the fang is hollow, like an hypodermic needle, with the venom duct leading into its base and the exit being located, not on the tip, but slightly on the forward edge near the tip (Plate 25). Often there is a replacement fang lying behind the functional one, ready for use in the event of the main one becoming broken or lost. The rest of the teeth are solid and do not have venom ducts leading to them. The fangs are hidden in a fleshy sheath that easily flattens out of the way under the pressure of biting. The marine acrochordid and natricines are non-venomous and have only solid teeth, none of which are enlarged as a fang.

The homalopsines, like some other colubrids, have a gland called Duvernoy's gland, which is different from the venom gland of hydrophiids and laticaudids. It is located in the upper jaw just above the rearmost teeth. These teeth are different from the solid, anterior teeth in that they are slightly grooved on the outer side (Figure 9.2). Duvernoy's gland discharges its secretion into a furrow running along the lateral edges of the rear teeth; the venom then follows the grooves, by capillary action, into the wound of a bitten animal. Although snakes with this kind of venom apparatus lack true fangs in the sense of hollow hypodermic-like teeth, they are referred to as 'rear-fanged'. In some, the grooved teeth in the rear are larger than the more anterior ones. A few rear-fanged species are dangerous to humans but none of the homalopsines are reported to be so.

The first stage in the evolutionary development of the venom apparatus probably was an enlargement of the teeth which allowed for deeper penetration of saliva into prey. A further refinement was the presence of grooves in the teeth; these facilitated introduction of a greater amount of saliva by capillary action, as still occurs in rear-fanged colubrids. The third stage was an enlargement of the grooves and curvature of their edges to form a channel through which venom could flow, thereby improving the efficiency of delivery and increasing the amount of venom injected. Finally, the meeting of the curved edges of the tooth formed a fang with a central canal.

THE NATURE OF VENOM

Snake venom is a complex solution of many different substances, including various kinds of toxins, each exerting its own effect. The kinds and combinations of toxins determine the overall action on the victim. Each species of snake has a different set of toxins and, when similar ones occur in different species, they may be mixed in different proportions. The action of each species' venom is therefore unique.

Further complicating this already complex situation is the fact that the effect of one toxin may be modified by the presence of another one. Two toxins operating together may produce effects additional to the sum of their independent ones, a phenomenon called synergism. Despite the diversity of toxins, their occurrence in different combinations and their synergistic effects, their action is not haphazard. Closely related species usually, but not always, have venoms rather similar to each other compared to species that are more distantly related. This fact has importance in the treatment of snake bite (see Chapter 10). Comparable (homologous) toxins in different species may differ only by the substitution of one or a few amino acids by other amino acids in the protein or peptide molecule.

Before proceeding to further discussion of the venoms themselves, it is necessary to provide some basic information about their major components. There are more than 20 amino acids produced biologically. These join together in various combinations to produce long, sometimes interconnected, molecular chains of great complexity. The smaller molecules, made up of groups of amino acids, are called peptides or, if somewhat larger, polypeptides. The still larger ones are called proteins and are a major component of protoplasm, blood serum and other biologically important substances, including snake venom.

Some of the more chemically active proteins are called enzymes. Each enzyme catalyses a very specific chemical reaction and under the right conditions will cause that reaction to proceed at a very rapid rate. Enzymes are necessary for carrying out nearly all of life's processes and without them no organism could live. Some enzymes contribute to chemical reactions leading to the synthesis of substances, whereas others are involved in breaking them down into simpler ones. It is the latter that predominates in venoms.

There are about 25 different kinds of enzymes found in the venoms of snakes. Not all of them are found in any one species and some are not found in any of the venomous marine ones. Some of the enzymes in venom have little or no toxic effect; others are highly toxic.

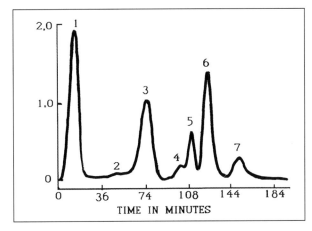

Figure 9.3
Chromatogram showing the relative amounts of seven fractions of the venom of *Aipysurus laevis*. Different substances move at different rates and separate out at different times. The vertical axis is a relative scale such that the area under the peak is proportional to the amount of substance present. High peaks represent major components, low peaks more minor ones.

The most important general classes of toxic enzymes in snake venoms are the proteases and the nucleotidases that digest tissues (more important in vipers than in venomous sea snakes) and the phospholipases that damage cell membranes. The hyaluronidases, while not directly toxic themselves, are referred to as 'spreading factors'. By causing hydrolysis of hyaluronic acid they facilitate diffusion of toxins into the tissues of the victim.

Not all of the toxins in venom are enzymes. Some are non-enzymatic proteins or polypeptides, usually of rather low molecular weight.

The toxins contained in sea snake venoms fall into several main categories based on the type of damage they cause. There are neurotoxins (that affect the nerves), haemotoxins (that affect the blood), myotoxins (that affect the muscles) and nephrotoxins (that affect the kidneys). Many land snakes contain primarily haemotoxins and myotoxins. In the cobra family (Elapidae) and in their close relatives, the venomous sea snakes (Hydrophiidae and Laticaudidae), neurotoxins often are the principal agents. Kenneth Zimmerman and various colleagues separated the venom of *Aipysurus laevis* into seven of its major components or fractions (Figure 9.3). Fraction 6 was highly lethal and was neurotoxic but fractions 1, 3 and 5 also were neurotoxic. Fractions 4 and 7 were myotoxic. Individual fractions displayed unusual effects, probably because in isolation they were freed from inhibition or synergistic influences of other compounds present in whole venom.

NEUROTOXINS

The area of contact between a nerve and a muscle is called the neuromuscular junction and it is there that some snake neurotoxins produce their effect. For a muscle to contract, it must receive stimulation from a nerve. At the end of the nerve are small cavities or vesicles in which a substance called acetylcholine is produced. When an electrical impulse travelling down the nerve reaches the end, it stimulates the release of acetylcholine which then diffuses across the neuromuscular junction to the membrane of the adjacent muscle where it attaches and stimulates muscle contraction. If the transmission of acetylcholine is blocked, the muscle is effectively paralysed. Snake toxins do that but in two different ways, depending on the particular toxins involved. All neurotoxins isolated from sea snakes to date have been polypeptides. Some affect the membranes on the nerve side of the junction. Under the electron microscope, the membrane appears wrinkled into cup-shaped folds called omega shapes. In this state, the vesicles cannot release their acetylcholine.

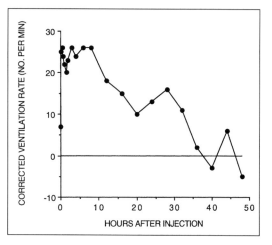

Other neurotoxins allow release of acetycholine but block its transmission by affecting the membrane on the muscle side of the junction. These toxins bind themselves to the specific places where acetycholine normally would attach and do not allow it to perform its function. Both kinds of neurotoxins may be found in the venom of a single species.

Neurotoxins act rapidly and, following the bite of a strongly neurotoxic snake, often are the immediate cause of death. Death in mammals may be caused by respiratory failure when neurotoxins cause paralysis of the muscles of the diaphragm that control breathing. Death in fish following envenomation by sea snakes also may be through asphyxiation. Kenneth Zimmerman, one of my PhD students, found that the venom of *Aipysurus laevis* paralysed the muscles controlling the pumping of water across the gills. The movements of the gill cover (operculum) became erratic and eventually ceased, preventing the fish from getting sufficient oxygen. Fish injected with venom exhibited progressive impairment of locomotion, balance and ventilation (pumping movements by the operculum). Initially there was an increase in ventilation but this soon was followed by marked reduction and eventually cessation (Figure 9.4). Inability of a fish to right itself or to coordinate its swimming movements would make it easier for a snake to overpower it.

Subduing or killing prey seems to be the primary function of neurotoxins as they have no major role in digestion. Neurotoxins are more prominent in the venoms of the venomous sea snakes and the land snakes of the cobra family (Elapidae), whereas, with a few exceptions, they are relatively less important in land snakes such as vipers.

Figure 9.4
Change in the 'breathing rate' (ventilation rate of the gills) of an eel, *Gymnothorax hepaticus*, following injection with venom of the banded sea krait (*Laticauda colubrina*). The ventilation rate is expressed as the number of ventilations per minute above or below the average ventilation rate of the same eel prior to injection (shown as a zero-level line).

Myotoxins

Myotoxins are enzymes that directly break down muscle fibres (Figure 9.5). Phospholipases are one of the important kinds of such enzymes. They cause the phospholipids that hold together the membranes of muscle cells to break down into fatty acids and

Figure 9.5
An electron microscopic photograph of the sternohyoideus muscle of a gold-fish.
Left: Normal muscle, bar = 0.65 μm .
Right: Muscle from a fish envenomated with venom from the olive sea snake (*Aipysurus laevis*); bar = 0.50μm. Note swelling of the terminal cisternae, hyaline degeneration (breakdown of the lattice structure of the muscle fibres) and disruption of banding. (Photographs courtesy Kenneth Zimmerman)

lysophospholipids. The damaged cells release, among other things, creatine kinase and a muscle protein called myoglobin. The appearance of large amounts of either of these substances in either the blood or urine is an indication that envenomation is serious (see Chapter 10).

Myotoxins usually act more slowly than neurotoxins. They play less of a role in the immobilisation of prey but a more prominent one in digestion.

HAEMOTOXINS

Haemotoxins affect the blood in two ways. Phospholipases break down the membranes of blood cells and release not myoglobin as in muscles but the respiratory pigment haemoglobin which may appear in the urine. Other enzymes interfere with the clotting properties of the blood. Haemotoxins are characteristic of vipers. In sea snake venoms haemotoxins seldom cause extensive damage and are of much less importance than are neurotoxins and myotoxins.

NEPHROTOXINS

Shantay Zimmerman, another of my PhD students, discovered that *Aipysurus laevis* has toxins that specifically affect the kidneys. Such toxins are called nephrotoxins. Mice injected with such low doses of venom that they survive the neurotoxic effects, develop severe kidney damage, beginning with inflammation within an hour, followed by death of kidney tissue within a week and eventually the appearance of large holes in the kidneys (Figure 9.6).

It is unlikely that nephrotoxins are involved in the subjugation or digestion of prey because of the length of time for severe damage to occur. However, this finding has important medical implications for human envenomations.

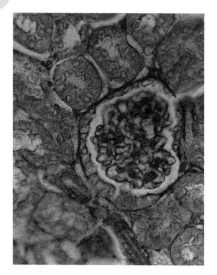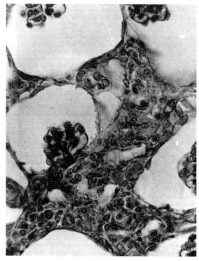

Figure 9.6
Comparison of the
kidney of a normal
mouse (left) and
the kidney from a
mouse one month
after injection with
0.025 mg/kg of
venom from the
olive sea snake,
Aipysurus laevus.
(Photograph
courtesy of Shantay
Zimmerman)

WHY ARE THERE VENOMOUS SEA SNAKES?

It was shown above that venoms are very complex chemically and that the muscles and teeth involved in their delivery are highly modified structures. How did such a complicated system evolve? The simple answer to this question is that sea snakes and sea kraits both inherited their venom and associated delivery apparatus from venomous ancestors, the elapid snakes. Similarly, the mildly venomous homalopsines have other colubrid relatives that share their venomous nature. However, this is only part of the answer and the ultimate reason must be sought in why venoms evolved in snakes in the first place.

Many people assume that the primary function of snake venom is defence and that venom and its delivery apparatus evolved in response to selection for protective devices. This is probably not true. It is much more likely that venom first arose in the role of facilitating feeding. That is still one of its primary functions. To explain the significance of snake venom, I first need to digress and consider some other features of the biology of snakes generally, especially limblessness and the morphology of the teeth.

Snakes arose from limbed reptiles. Indeed, in pythons tiny spurs protruding from the side of the body remain as relics of former hindlimbs. Many present-day lizards of several families show various tendencies toward limblessness, ranging from species that have their limbs only slightly reduced in size, through those that have tiny, nearly useless ones, to those that have lost all external evidence of them. The last are commonly mistaken for snakes. Except for pythons, snakes have completely lost not only their limbs but even the internal bones (girdles) that provide support for limbs in other vertebrates.

Once snakes completely lost their limbs and the supporting girdles, these structures were never regained. As snakes invaded different habitats, they developed a variety of adaptations that suited them to new lifestyles.

Snakes' teeth are conical and effective in piercing. They are curved backwards so that once a prey is impaled, the only way it can dislodge itself is by moving towards the throat. The teeth are arranged in longitudinal rows in the roof of the mouth and on the lower jaw, and once a prey animal is free from the more anterior ones, it merely becomes impaled on those further back — clearly a counter-productive manoeuvre from the standpoint of the victim! Such teeth are effective in holding the prey and compensate for the loss of ability to restrain prey using forelimbs. However, piercing, recurved teeth do not have cutting or shearing edges, or grinding surfaces, and snakes cannot chew their food into smaller pieces. This attribute, combined with lack of limbs and claws, used by many vertebrates to tear or dismember prey, commits snakes to swallowing their food whole, and at that they are masters.

Snakes have kinetic skulls; that is, the bones are loosely connected and can move upon each other, giving the skull a great deal of flexibility. The right and left halves can move somewhat independently. While holding prey securely with the teeth on one side of the head, a snake can open its mouth wider on the other side and slide that part of the head forward and gain another purchase. Holding and moving forward by the two sides of the head alternately results in the snake literally stretching itself around the prey until the latter reaches the throat and can be swallowed. Ingestion of large items is aided by an ability to dislocate the lower jaws, thereby providing more room for the passage of food. In this way, and by stretching the skin, a snake can swallow animals with a girth larger than its own.

Such gastronomic feats are not possible for most vertebrates because the bony girdle that supports the anterior limbs encircles the oesophagous and, being firm and rigid, obstructs the passage of large food items.

SWALLOWING LARGE PREY

In a rather circuitous way, I have now outlined the consequences of limblessness for feeding in snakes. On the one hand, limblessness and type of dentition committed snakes to the swallowing of prey whole but on the other hand it made it possible for them to ingest exceptionally large items.

There are advantages in being able to eat large prey. In the face of infrequent availability of food, it is important to be able to eat whatever can be captured, regardless of size. By increasing the size range of animals that can be consumed, a wider selection of prey becomes available to the predator and food shortages are less likely to occur. Another consequence of eating large prey is that a single meal can last a long time, thereby reducing the amount of time and energy spent in foraging for food. The combination of large meals and low metabolic rates (see Chapters 4 and 8) means that snakes need to feed only infrequently and can maintain themselves on only a few meals per month or, if necessary, a few per year. However, there also are two disadvantages of eating large prey: the danger of being harmed by the prey, and indigestion. Venom helps reduce both risks.

Small animals, unless they have some particularly noxious quality (such as stinging, bad taste or being poisonous), can be grasped in the mouth and swallowed directly with relative impunity. However, with increasing size of prey, the relative strengths of the victim and the predator become more evenly matched. The likelihood of the prey inflicting physical damage upon the predator increases, either through thrashing about and breaking teeth or by biting, clawing or in other ways counter-attacking. For example, imagine yourself trying to swallow a vicious, sharp-toothed moray eel (as some laticaudids do) without the aid of hands or utensils. Some sea snakes eat fish with sharp, venomous spines that would seem to require special care in handling. In all cases of dealing with large, dangerous prey, it would be easier to swallow a dead or moribund animal than one that is still struggling. The introduction of a chemical agent into the saliva that quickly pacifies prey would be an obvious advantage. Selection for more powerful and quicker-acting killing agents probably led to the evolution of the neurotoxins in snake venoms.

It was probably only after venom had become quite powerful that it assumed its secondary role in defence. A weak substance having no immediate effect on an attacker would not seem to provide any advantage upon which selection could operate. Even today some sea snakes do not use their venom in a defensive capacity. Most species of *Laticauda*, although having highly potent venom which they use to subdue prey, seldom bite defensively, even after sustained and intense provocation. Also species that feed solely on fish eggs and have no need of venom for subjugating prey (see Chapter 4) have nearly lost the ability to produce it and have a degenerate venom apparatus, an unlikely development if defence were a primary function of venom.

Although homalopsines are not venomous to humans and they lack the complex venom-delivery system of the laticaudids and hydrophiids, their saliva does immobilise prey. Fish captured by *Cerberus rynchops* and held in its jaws sometimes exhibit dilation of the pupils and a darkening that spreads from the site of the bite. Fish retrieved from the jaws of these snakes often die.

DIGESTING LARGE PREY

Finely chewed food provides a very great surface area upon which digestive enzymes can operate and accordingly digestion proceeds rapidly. By contrast, the outer surface of the same amount of food in one large piece is relatively small. Digestion must proceed gradually from the surface inward. Again, imagine yourself in a situation comparable to that of a snake. You have just swallowed whole an entire ham and do not have recourse to medicines to treat indigestion.

Saliva functions in lubricating food and facilitating its swallowing. In addition, in most vertebrates saliva contains some weak enzymes that begin the process of digestion. In animals that chew their food, these enzymes are mixed thoroughly with the food during mastication. That advantage is denied to snakes. However, the penetration of the teeth into the prey during capture and ingestion introduces small quantitites of digestive enzymes, thereby exposing internal tissues to their action in at least a limited way.

The venom gland is merely a modified salivary gland that produces a much more powerful and chemically complex secretion (venom) than do other salivary glands. There is no clear demarcation between saliva and venom. Rather they represent two ends of a spectrum of toxicity and digestive effectiveness.

Snakes are carnivores and since meat is mostly protein, the most appropriate kind of enzyme to inject would be one that digests protein. This may explain the presence of proteolytic enzymes in snake venom. Both from the standpoint of digestion and subjugation of prey, there would be a selective advantage in having mechanisms that improve the penetration of saliva (venom) and also in increasing the power of the toxins it contains. The latter led to the evolution of venom, the former to the evolution of the injection apparatus (see pages 95-97, The Venom Apparatus).

The ultimate in venoms and delivery apparatus is the ability to inject a rapidly lethal substance, which is also a powerful digestive enzyme, deep into an animal. The circulatory system of the victim during the remaining short period of its life distributes the venom throughout its body, practically to every cell. In addition to killing it, the venom begins digesting the prey from within. Such internal digestion partly compensates for the digestive disadvantage of swallowing large, whole prey.

Most non-venomous snakes have weak digestive enzymes in their saliva. However, some so-called harmless snakes are not entirely so and have been implicated in human envenomations of varying severity. The saliva of these snakes has properties intermediate between those of truly harmless snakes and those of venomous ones. Whether such oral secretions are called saliva or weak venom is a matter of preference; they represent an intermediate stage along the evolutionary pathway towards increasing toxicity.

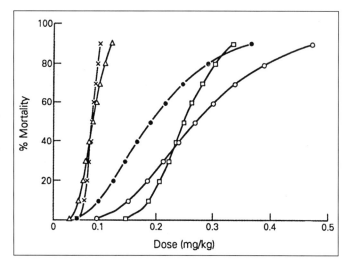

Figure 9.7 Susceptibility of different species of prey fish to various dosages of venom of the olive sea snake (*Aipysurus laevis*). Each curve represents a probit curve of the mortality of a particular species: circles = *Dascyllus aruanus*; dots = *Chromis nitida*; x's = *Chromis atripectoralis*; triangles = *Istiblennius meleagris*; squares = *Istiblenius edentulus*. *Istiblenius* are blennies and the other species are pomacentrids.

COEVOLUTION OF VENOM AND OF RESISTANCE BY PREY

Why is sea snake venom so extraordinarily toxic? Why should a sea snake, in a single bite, need to be able to deliver venom powerful enough to kill hundreds of mice or over 50 humans (see Chapter 10) Part of the answer may lie in the resistance of the target species toward which the venom is directed, that is, the prey fish. It is known that some of the lower terrestrial vertebrates are remarkably resistant to land snake venoms and it may be that fish are resistant to sea snake venom. It was this possibility that led me and some of my students, notably Kenneth Zimmerman, to compare the effect of sea snake venom on their natural prey with that on fish that were not part of their diet.

We injected venom of *Aipysurus laevis* into five species of prey fish (blennies and pomacentrids) and found that species differed in their susceptibility to it (Figure 9.7). The species that were least susceptible were those that were able to respire through their skin as well as through their gills and we reasoned that, since death from envenomation is caused by asphyxiation, perhaps the resistance was merely the ability to survive by way of cutaneous respiration until the fish recovered from the effect of neurotoxins on its ventilatory muscles.

Eels have exceptionally high capacities to respire through the skin so I decided to test the resistances of four species of New Guinean eels to the venom of their sea snake predators. Although some species did have extraordinarily high resistances to the venom, others were very sensitive. So resistance is not solely dependent upon the ability to respire through the skin. Rather it seemed to be related to the degree of contact between eels and snakes. Two species of eels of the genus *Gymnothorax* that were known to be prey of sea snakes were highly resistant, whereas two species of other genera that occurred in the same geographic areas as sea snakes but in different habitats and hence seldom, if ever, were eaten by them, were sensitive. Naomie Poran (a postdoctoral research fellow in my laboratory) and I tested a fifth species of eel from the Atlantic Ocean where sea snakes do not occur at all and found it to be extremely sensitive. We suggested that resistance by prey and toxicity of venom may be co-evolved attributes. That is, they depend upon selection operating on both predator and prey. There would be selection for increased toxicity of venom because rapid dispatch of prey would be an advantage for the predator. This increased toxicity in turn would serve as a selective force. Eels that developed increased resistance would have a better chance of surviving an encounter with a snake. This would see-saw back and forth in an evolutionary 'arms race' between predator and prey, resulting in continuing increase in toxicity on the part of snakes and progressive elevation of resistance on the part of eels.

There is another possible explanation for these results, however. Perhaps eels of the genus *Gymnothorax* were not susceptible to the sea snake venom because of a general hardiness, rather than because of a specific, co-evolved resistance. To test between these alternative hypotheses, Judy Powell and I examined the response of a species of *Gymnothorax* from the Caribbean where no sea snakes have ever occurred. The Caribbean *Gymnothorax*, in contrast to the New Guinean ones, were highly susceptible to sea snake venom. So the co-evolutionary hypothesis was supported; only those species of *Gymnothorax* whose distribution coincided with that of the snakes and were preyed upon by them were resistant, not the genus generally.

The resistance of prey may explain why sea snakes are so toxic to mice and humans. Venom powerful enough to overcome the co-evolved resistance of prey species may, in consequence, be overkill for other animals.

Another reason why venom may be so powerful is the need to kill prey quickly. Although a weak venom may kill a fish eventually, a more powerful one will do so more quickly, thereby reducing both the risk of injury to the snake by a counter-attacking prey and the likelihood of the prey escaping before being incapacitated.

The study of the effects of the venom of sea snakes on natural prey is one of the most neglected but at the same time one of the most biologically important aspects of sea snake toxicology. There is great scope for further research in this field.

SEA SNAKES AND HUMANS

Humans traditionally fear snakes of all kinds and tend to evaluate their interaction with them as negative, with humans being the injured party. Indeed in Judaeo-Christian mythology, a snake is cast as the original embodiment of evil and the architect of all subsequent human woes. The relationship is not entirely one-sided, however. Humans kill many more snakes than snakes kill humans and in fact about 80 per cent of snake bites sustained by humans are received while engaging in that activity.

Most people are fascinated by snakes. To naturalists they are creatures of grace and beauty; to scientists they are subjects of study; to some small boys, they are personal pets and objects with which to equalise their standing in the adult world; to many they add delicious horror to jungle movies; and to some they provide eroticism to Madame X's unspeakable sideshow act.

Animals with such broad-based appeal contribute substantially to culture. It is one of the positive aspects of their relationship with humans. In addition to contributing in the above ways, sea snakes have provided practical benefits to humans. They have been exploited for a number of reasons.

USES OF SEA SNAKES

Sea snakes are used for food, leather and medicines, and in some localities industries have developed around catching and processing them for human exploitation.

LEATHER

Reptilian leather has been much in demand for stylish products, especially belts, wallets, watch bands and handbags, and occasionally for jackets, ties, briefcases and shoes. Sea snake leather has been part of that trade.

Local leathercraft from sea snakes has been produced on a small scale in the Philippines since about 1930, initially involving primarily file snakes but later expanding to sea kraits and hydrophiids. In 1973 there was a promotion of these products in tourist shops in Manila. The monthly volume of trade was estimated at about 2000 pieces made from *Acrochordus granulatus*, 5000 from various *Laticauda* species and 1500 from species of *Hydrophis*.

Commercial export of sea snakes from the Philippines was begun on a large scale in 1934 by the Japanese who set up processing plants and taught local people how to catch and treat the product. Most of the skins were sent as salted rawhide to Japan where they were tanned and re-exported to Europe as 'Japanese sea snake leather'.

There is now more local control over the industry. In 1973 the estimated catch was somewhat less than 50 000 per month. However, the market fluctuates rather widely with the changing dictates of fashion and in the future it may diminish because public objection to reptilian leather on conservational grounds seems to be increasing. The main species involved in the export trade from the Philippines are *Laticauda semifasciata*, *Laticauda laticaudata* and *Hydrophis ornatus*.

The Ryukyu Islands of Japan also have a thriving sea snake industry based primarily on species of *Laticauda*. No official figures are available on the volume of trade but I visited one of the main processing plants (Plate 27) and observed about 1000 specimens, mostly *Laticauda semifasciata*, received in a single day. Shipments are not received daily, however, and the annual intake was not divulged. In the interests of conservation, eggs are taken from harvested females and incubated to hatching and the young released in the sea.

In Australia a cottage industry of products from sea snake leather expanded into a commercial enterprise in 1977; it became regulated by governmental licenses in 1986. The principal source of supply is the by-catch from prawn trawling, mainly in the Gulf of Carpentaria.

FOOD

Sea snakes are exploited for food either raw, smoked or cooked. In the Ryukyus at least some of the meat obtained as a consequence of the leather industry is used for human consumption. Meat and sometimes eggs from gravid females are eaten in various Asian countries. Sea snake meat is believed sometimes to be mixed with fish meat and sold as tinned fish. A restaurant on Iriomote Island in the Ryukyus has a stew of pork feet and the meat and skin of *Laticauda semifasciata* as the specialty of the house. Many Asians believe snake meat to be an aphrodisiac and consume it for that reason. In Manila a restaurant that specialises in aphrodisiac food includes sea snake dishes on its menu.

Sea snake meat also is used for domestic animal feed. In the Philippines carcasses arising from the leather industry are used to prepare feed for poultry and pigs, and in other places snakes may be indiscriminately included in 'fish meal' for stock.

Sea snake fat is rendered for oil that is used in making margarines or 'butter' in some countries. It also has industrial uses including the softening of sea snake leather.

MEDICINE

Snakes have long been considered to be medicinal. Alcoholic spirits made from snakes, particularly from their gall, are widely believed in the Orient to have health-giving properties and to bestow sexual virility.

In the West both homeopathic and allopathic medicine made use of venoms, or their components, in the treatment of at least fifty diseases and maladies, including leprosy, epilepsy, haemorrhage and venous thrombosis, and as pain killers in cases of incurable cancer and other severely painful conditions. Venoms have been used in pregnancy tests and the diagnosis of syphilis and schizophrenia. Most of these uses have been abandoned. In some cases venom was found not to have the properties attributed to it. In others there were undesirable side effects and in still others the use of venom simply was superseded by easier, cheaper or more efficient treatments. Terrestrial snakes were featured more prominently than sea snakes in the traditional reptilian pharmacopoeia. However, the more modern and more valuable uses of venom include those from sea snakes.

Venoms are rich sources of a number of biochemically and medically important enzymes that are not easily obtained elsewhere. They can be used to cleave complex molecules into simpler, more easily identified compounds and in this way contribute to an understanding of the chemical structure of such substances. Venoms are valuable tools in the study of the structure of viruses, including some that are agents of leukemia.

The very specific and sometimes unique action of snake venoms upon cell membranes or on the neuromuscular junction (see Chapter 9) means that they can be used experimentally to block specific physiological processes, thereby allowing scientists to learn more about normal function of nerves and muscles. Some snake venoms are used in the study of the regeneration of muscle fibres and are important in research into muscular disorders.

In recent years there have been many advances in the study of sea snake venoms using genetic manipulation and the cloning of the DNA that organises the synthesis of toxins. In some cases bacteria have been engineered to produce snake toxins. Such research is leading to a much greater understanding of the precise structure of toxin molecules and of how the different parts of the molecule function in producing toxic effects. Mutant toxins can be produced or existing toxins slightly modified to assess how small differences in molecular structure alter toxic properties. Previously unsuspected toxins have been discovered in some snake venoms. This new information also has practical value by leading to better ways of treating and immunising against venoms.

Because of their importance in basic biochemical and medical research, and the danger and difficulty associated in obtaining them, some sea snake venoms are among the most expensive materials for their weight in the world. A catalogue from a chemical supply company for 1996 listed the range in price for dry sea snake venom as US$11.78 to US$17.15 per milligram. To put these prices into more familiar terms, the most expensive one costs more than US$17 million per kilogram of dry venom!

Lest the reader be tempted to embark on a 'get rich quick' scheme to sell sea snake venom, it should be emphasised that the amount of venom that can be extracted from a sea snake is small and then it must be freeze-dried, leaving only a minute quantity of dry venom. Large numbers of snakes must be milked in order to obtain a marketable quantity. Suppliers will purchase only from a recognised specialist in order to ensure that they are getting venom from the species designated, so not only training in snake-handling but expertise in the science of herpetology is a prerequisite. All things considered, including the large difference in the price suppliers pay for venom compared to that at which they sell it, milking sea snakes for venom is not more lucrative than other professions, just more dangerous.

MARINE SNAKES AS A SUSTAINABLE RESOURCE

Between 1984 and 1987 Glen Burns and I carried out a study of sea snake populations for the Australian National Parks and Wildlife

Service. The purpose of the study was to evaluate the impact of humans on sea snake populations and to assess the feasibility of harvesting sea snakes as a sustainable resource. Since then additional basic research on sea snake populations has been published (especially by Harold Voris and his colleagues) that adds to an understanding of what the responses of sea snakes to exploitation might be. The basic biology impinging on this topic was reviewed in Chapter 6. Here the data will be evaluated in terms of its implication for the commercial harvesting of snakes and the directions that should be taken to conserve this resource.

The population characteristics of marine snakes vary from one species to another in important ways. Furthermore, even within a particular species basic attributes may vary geographically. Population data are available from only a few species and currently it is unwise to form sweeping generalisations for application to marine snakes as a whole or to any species in all of its distributional range. More comparative studies are needed and effective management plans will require detailed study of the populations targeted for exploitation. However, some emergent properties are becoming apparent that warrant discussion.

One extreme along the spectrum of reproductive strategies consists of slow-growing, late-maturing individuals that reproduce infrequently but live a long time so that over an extended period considerable numbers of offspring are produced. The other extreme consists of rapid-growing, early-maturing individuals that have high fecundity and produce large numbers of young in one breeding season.

Among the marine snakes studied to date, there are a few that appear to be of the second kind. For example, *Astrotia stokesii*, *Enhydrina schistosa* and *Hydrophis elegans* have unusually high fecundity and the homalopsine *Bitia hydroides* matures early. Such species would be expected to be able to repair population losses relatively quickly and be resilient to harvesting. However, at least one of these (*Enhydrina schistosa*) suffers very high mortality among the young and few females survive to sexual maturity so this species may be more vulnerable than it would at first appear.

Most of the sea snakes that have been studied tend toward the first strategy. In one of the better-studied species, *Aipysurus laevis*, females only mature after 4–5 years, then breed only on alternate years and on average produce small broods (average brood size = 2.6). There are few small animals in the population but longevity is about 15 years. Such species cannot recover quickly from depletion of their populations. The harvesting of adults impinges upon reproduction for many years into the future and replacement is slow. They would be expected to be especially vulnerable to exploitation. Harvesting of the larger females would have a greater immediate effect upon reproduction as such animals produce larger broods than do smaller females.

It is unlikely that exploited populations of *Aipysurus laevis* would be replenished by migration of excess individuals from undepleted populations. Given its low reproductive rate and the low numbers of juveniles in the population, there would be few juveniles to disperse. Adults are very sedentary and occupy small home ranges. Consequently replenishment of a depleted area by migration from unexploited populations would be slow.

Because some species have characteristics that would seem to make them highly vulnerable to exploitation (e.g. *Aipysurus laevis*), whereas others, such as *Enhydrina schistosa* and *Hydrophis elegans*, may be more resilient, a single approach is not applicable to all species. It is important in formulating a management plan that differences among species be taken into account and different quotas applied.

Some species with high fecundity may nevertheless occur in low population densities and should not have high quotas. *Astrotia stokesii* is one such species. Despite its high fecundity it is relatively uncommon in many localities. *Lapemis curtus* has intermediate average fecundity (9 young per clutch), yet in the Gulf of Carpentaria it is one of the more abundant species and could probably sustain a somewhat greater harvesting rate than other species of equivalent clutch size.

In the 1991 prawn season about 119 600 sea snakes were taken as by-catch of trawling. This catch is more than the annual number licensed by the Queensland Fisheries (20 000 in 1987) to be taken by the skinning industry. So the by-catch from prawn trawling in the Gulf of Carpentaria could fill quotas. However, it was estimated that only about 40 per cent of the snakes brought up in trawls would die if returned to the water. So harvesting the entire by-catch kills 60 per cent more snakes than would die if the snakes were released; that is, harvesting the snakes would somewhat more than double the current impact of trawling, assuming that the number of trawlers stays the same and trawling procedures are not altered (such as trawling areas known to have abundant sea snakes on days when prawn catches are light).

Trawling for fin-fish is less likely to have an impact upon sea snake populations because most such trawling uses nets with larger mesh size and takes place in deeper water where there are fewer snakes.

The aggregation of *Laticauda* species on islands make them especially vulnerable to capture in large numbers. At any one time up to 75–85 per cent of an entire population may be concentrated ashore in a small area.

A few guidelines for management of marine snakes seem appropriate.

1. It would seem unwise to increase the harvesting rate of populations presently subjected to pressure from trawling.

2. All aspects of sea snake biology should be considered in formulating a management scheme. For example, *Enhydrina schistosa* might be more vulnerable to exploitation than its high fecundity rate would suggest. Assessment of its capacity for harvesting needs to be tempered by its very high mortality rate and high infertility.

3. A management policy for sea snakes should take account of differences among species and of the high vulnerability of some species to exploitation. For example, species should not be harvested when large numbers of females are carrying young. Because of interspecific differences in breeding season, the restricted season may need to be different for different species. Because of intraspecific geographic variation in reproductive cycle, the restricted season for a particular species may need to be different at different localities. The aseasonality of breeding of some species also needs to be taken into account. There should not be blanket quotas but rather separate quotas for different species and at different times of year, with some species completely protected.

Commercial harvesting is not the only threat to sea snakes. Anslem de Silva listed four categories of human-induced environmental hazards faced by sea snakes in Sri Lanka. These apply to other regions as well. They are:

1. rapid reduction of mangrove swamps for firewood, aquaculture and human settlement
2. industrial pollution of coastal waters and estuaries
3. death and depletion of coral reefs
4. depletion of snakes' food resources by overfishing.

HOW DANGEROUS ARE SEA SNAKES?

Some of the most frequently asked questions regarding sea snakes are 'How dangerous are they?' and 'Are they more dangerous than land snakes?' There is no simple, unequivocal answer to either question.

Table 10.1

Attributes of some sea snakes in relation to their danger to humans

Species	Fang Length (mm)	Venom Yield (mg)	Mean Toxicity (LD_{50} mice; mg/kg)	Temperament	Known Human Fatalities
Acalyptophis peronii	—	0.33	0.08	Bites if provoked	—
Aipysurus duboisii	1.80	0.43	0.04	Bites when handled; may attack	—
Aipysurus eydouxii	1.34	0.60	11.70	Reluctant to bite	—
Aipysurus foliosquama	—	0.48	—	—	—
Aipysurus laevis	3.96 (4.70)	7.50 (33)	0.22	Bites if provoked	—
Astrotia stokesii	6.70	31.30 (152)	0.35	Aggressive when disturbed; bites repeatedly	—
Disteira major	3.80	22.80	0.19	—	—
Emydocephalus annulatus	0.15	—	>26.00	Reluctant to bite	—
Enhydrina schistosa	3.70	8.50 (79)	0.14	Easily angered; aggressive	Yes
Hydrophis brooki	—	1.10	—	—	—
Hydrophis coggeri	—	0.13	0.18	Bites if provoked	—
Hydrophis cyanocinctus	—	8.20 (80)	1.24	Bites readily	Yes
Hydrophis elegans	2.60 (3.90)	7.20 (24)	0.27	—	—
Hydrophis fasciatus	—	—	<0.18	—	—
Hydrophis klossi	—	1.00	—	Rarely bites spontaneously	—
Hydrophis melanosoma	—	—	0.40	Rarely bites spontaneously	—
Hydrophis ornatus	—	8.30	0.16	—	Yes
Hydrophis spiralis	—	2.10	—	Easily angered; aggressive	Yes
Kerilia jerdoni	—	2.80	—	Rarely bites spontaneously	—
Lapemis curtus	3.30	3.80 (15)	0.62	Aggressive if molested	Yes
Laticauda colubrina	—	10.60	0.42	Extremely reluctant to bite	—
Laticauda laticaudata	—	—	0.17	Extremely reluctant to bite	—
Laticauda semifasciata	—	2.50	0.50	Reluctant to bite	—
Pelamis platurus	1.50	1.40 (2.80)	0.28	Bites if provoked	Yes
Thalassophis anomalus	—	—	—	—	Yes

Note: Single values are means (with unusually large maxima in parentheses), either of individual values of a particular study or of grand means of multiple studies.

The threat a venomous snake poses is dependent on a number of factors, including its aggressiveness, the length of its fangs, the toxicity of its venom and the dosage delivered. A snake that steadfastly refuses to bite defensively is not dangerous to a molester, regardless of how toxic the venom may be. A highly aggressive snake with venom of low toxicity may be more of a threat than a more venomous, but tranquil, one. A snake that delivers a massive dose of weak venom may be potentially more dangerous than one that gives a smaller dose of more potent venom. A long fang that delivers its venom deep into the victim's body is more dangerous than a shorter one inflicting a more superficial wound, other factors being equal. However, a short-fanged species with highly toxic venom may be more dangerous than a longer-fanged but less toxic one. These few examples provide an idea of the complexity involved in evaluating the potential danger of any particular species. Table 10.1 provides data on the attributes of sea snakes that are relevant to their potential danger to humans.

TOXICITY

Ethical considerations prevent deliberately testing the effects of sea snake venoms on humans and available information on toxicity has come from imprecise clinical data or from experiments on laboratory animals, especially rats and mice. However, humans and other mammalian species may respond differently to venoms, as do different species of the natural prey of snakes (see Chapter 9) and therefore laboratory animals serve only as approximate models for human envenomation. Furthermore, different species of laboratory animals may respond differently to venom. A particular species may be highly susceptible to the venom of one kind of snake but much less so to that of another, with the reverse ranking being true for a different species of victim. Nevertheless experiments on laboratory animals have produced information not available otherwise and certain conclusions can be drawn.

One is that the site of injection (intramuscular, intravenous or intraperitoneal) influences the nature and timing of symptoms. Another is that the method of handling and preparing venom affects its action. A third is that the age and health of the victim influences its susceptibility to envenomation. Finally, there are differences in the toxicity of venom produced, even by the same individual snake at different seasons, in different states of health or at different ages.

Not all species have been studied with the same degree of intensity or rigour and consequently data are more precise and reliable for some species than for others.

Despite these sources of error, some interesting points are evident.

There is a wide range of toxicities of venom among sea snakes with a difference between weakest to most powerful of over 500 fold. The species with the most toxic venom (for mice) are *Acalyptophis peronii* and *Aipysurus duboisii* with LD$_{50}$s of less than 0.1 mg/kg (Table 10.1). Then, there is a group of somewhat less potent ones that include *Enhydrina schistosa, Disteira major, Hydrophis ornatus, Hydrophis fasciatus, Hydrophis coggeri* and *Laticauda laticaudata* with LD$_{50}$s between 0.1 and 0.2. Most of the species have venom with intermediate LD$_{50}$s (between 0.2 and 0.7 mg/kg) with one, *Hydrophis cyanocinctus*, having somewhat weaker venom (LD$_{50}$=1.24 mg/kg). Finally, there are two egg-eating species, *Aipysurus eydouxii* and *Emydocephalus annulatus*, with very weak venom (LD$_{50}$s about 10–30 mg/kg).

DOSE DELIVERED

Sea snakes, like land snakes, can deliver or withhold venom at will and in some species about 70 per cent of bites to humans are blank, that is, no venom is delivered and no symptoms develop. That percentage may well vary markedly among species of snake.

The amount of venom obtained by milking sea snakes can give a rough indication of their potential delivery. Massaging the venom gland during milking probably stimulates a greater release of venom than would occur during real bites and probably exaggerates the normal dose injected. However, some comparisons can be made.

In general, sea snakes have highly toxic venom delivered in rather small doses. Most venomous sea snakes deliver less venom than do many dangerous land snakes. Of the species for which venom yields have been studied, some species deliver on average less than 1 milligram of venom; these include a variety of taxa but includes the egg-eater *Aipysurus eydouxii*. Most species have intermediate mean yields of about 1–10 milligrams. Two species, *Disteira major* and *Astrotia stokesii*, have exceptionally large mean venom yields: more than 20 milligrams.

In comparison to venomous land snakes, these venom yields are low. Almost all of the large, dangerous terrestrial snakes, such as the kraits, cobras, large Australian elapids and the large vipers, have venom yields in excess of 30 milligrams and some have yields as high as several hundred milligrams. In some sea snakes maximum venom yields are considerably higher than mean yields and extend into the range of yields of large terrestrial snakes. For example, *Astrotia stokesii* has a maximum yield of more than 150 milligrams and *Enhydrina schistosa* and *Hydrophis cyanocinctus* sometimes produce as much as about 80 milligrams (Table 10.1).

It is important to know not only how much venom is delivered with a single bite (Plate 28) but also whether successive bites are likely to deliver multiple doses. Again, species differ. Olive sea snakes (*Aipysurus laevis*) delivered substantial doses only on the first 'bite'. A second milking sometimes yielded a small amount of venom but the third one was nearly always dry. In contrast, *Astrotia stokesii* (Figure 10.1) yielded massive and approximately equal doses of venom for seven consecutive 'bites', the amount decreasing only on the eighth one. This observation has clinical significance; a small child treading on a snake of this species in shallow water was bitten 11 times in rapid succession and survived only because of quick, appropriate medical treatment (see page 126, Human Fatalities from Sea Snake Bites).

Figure 10.1
The author milking the venom from an *Astrotia stokesii* by letting it bite a rubber membrane stretched over a glass beaker. The venom is extruded into the beaker. (Photograph courtesy of Ben Cropp)

HUMAN LETHAL DOSE

Only a few species of sea snakes commonly bite and kill humans (Table 10.1). How dangerous a venom is to humans depends on a combination of its toxicity to the recipient and the amount delivered. Both of these topics have been discussed already. Now, it remains to evaluate their combined effects.

Most species of sea snakes for which information is available are potentially harmful, the average dose of venom delivered in most cases exceeding the estimated human lethal dose (Table 10.2). Given the known high toxicities (at least to mice) of hydrophiid and laticaudid venoms and the quantities delivered, all but the egg-eaters should be considered as potentially lethal and should be treated with respect.

Enhydrina schistosa, a species responsible for many human deaths, has a maximum delivery of about 53 times as much as is required to kill a person or, put another way, a maximum dose could kill 53 people! This value is over six-fold higher than the most deadly vipers and twice as high as for maximum yields of king cobra, death adder and Australian brown snake venoms. Only the tiger snake is known to be capable of delivering a more deadly bite.

However, Table 10.2 may not contain the deadliest of either the land or sea snakes. Two terrestrial snakes from Australia, the fierce snake (*Oxyuranus microlepidotus*) and the taipan (*Oxyuranus scutellatus*), are suspected of being more dangerous than any of the terrestrial species listed in Table 10.2 and in fact some herpetologists claim the fierce snake to be the deadliest snake in the world.

Table 10.2

Comparison of the potential deadliness to humans of sea snakes and some of the most dangerous land snakes

Species	No. of humans that could be killed by a:	
	Mean Yield	Maximum Yield
SEA SNAKES		
Beaked Sea Snake (*Enhydrina schistosa*)	5.67	52.67
Hardwick's Sea Snake (*Lapemis curtus*)	1.90	6.50
Blue-belted Sea Snake (*Hydrophis cyanocinctus*)	1.56	2.00
Elegant Sea Snake (*Hydrophis elegans*)	0.47	1.27
Yellow-bellied Sea Snake (*Pelamis platurus*)	0.40	0.80
DANGEROUS LAND SNAKES		
ELAPIDAE		
King Cobra (*Ophiophagus hannah*}	21.05	25.00
Tiger Snake (*Notechis scutatus*)	11.67	63.00
Asian Cobra (*Naja naja*)	9.66	34.86
Death Adder (*Acanthopis antarcticus*)	7.80	23.60
Spitting Cobra (*Naja nigricollis*)	6.11	7.78
Indian Krait (*Bungarus caeruleus*)	4.00	4.80
Green Mamba (*Dendroaspis angusticeps*)	1.17	6.33
Australian Brown Snake (*Pseudonaja textilis*)	0.80	26.80
VIPERIDAE		
Saw-scaled Viper (*Echis carinatus*)	7.50	8.75
Gaboon Viper (*Bitis gabonica*)	5.83	6.67
Mojave Rattlesnake (*Crotalus scutulatus*)	5.60	7.20
Brazilian Rattlesnake (*Crotalus durissus*)	3.00	4.00
Bushmaster (*Lachesis mutus*)	2.91	3.64
Russell's Viper (*Viper russelli*)	2.82	3.70
Fer-de-lance (*Bothrops atrox*)	2.73	3.64
Timber Rattlesnake (*Crotalus horridus*)	1.71	2.29
Cottonmouth Moccasin (*Agkistrodon piscivorus*)	1.00	1.20
COLUBRIDAE		
Boomslang (*Dispholidus typus*)	1.20	1.60

Note: Figures have been calculated by dividing the mean or maximum venom yield by the estimated human lethal dose.

A number of sea snakes not listed in Table 10.2 are nearly as toxic to mice as is *Enhydrina schistosa* and at least two species, *Acalyptophis peronii* and *Aipysurus duboisii*, are considerably more so (Table 10.1). Consequently, these species and possibly others may be as dangerous to humans as is *Enhydrina*. This cannot be verified, however, until there are clinical data on envenomation of humans by these species.

The data in Table 10.2 indicate the potential lethality of maximum deliveries of venom. However, average deliveries are lower than maximum ones, often considerably so in sea snakes, and the pattern is altered if average yields are used. Then, *Enhydrina schistosa* ranks not as the second-most deadly but as the sixth in comparison to elapids and as second in comparison to vipers. Note, however, that it still outranks such formidable snakes as kraits, the green mamba, the Gaboon viper and the bushmaster. Most of the sea snakes rank below the most deadly of the land snakes but are on a par with some of the rattlesnakes and the cottonmouth moccasin (Table 10.2).

In conclusion, the most dangerous of the sea snakes rank among the deadliest of the land snakes. Except for *Aipysurus eydouxii* and species of *Emydocephalus* that feed exclusively on fish eggs and have weak venom, all sea snakes should be considered potentially lethal.

FANG LENGTH

Among the venomous marine snakes, the development of the feeding apparatus is related to the size of prey eaten. Species that take large prey tend to have a wider gape to the mouth and longer fangs than those that eat smaller items. The species that eat fish eggs have small fangs; in *Emydocephalus* species they are so small as to be hardly functional.

Most of the sea snakes for which data are available have fangs of less than 4 millimetres in length. The only exceptions are *Aipysurus laevis* (fang lengths up to 4.7 millimetres) and *Astrotia stokesii* (fangs of 6.7 millimetres) (Table 10.1). The largest individuals of *A. laevis* can just penetrate a wet suit when biting, and *A. stokesii* can consistently do so.

Those sea snakes with the longest fangs are comparable with some of the dangerous Australian terrestrial elapids (fang lengths are 3.5 millimetres in tiger snakes, 4.2 millimetres in brown snakes and 7.4 millimetres in death adders) but have shorter fangs than those of the taipan (12.5 millimetres) and are much less impressive than the large vipers: the diamondback rattlesnake's fangs are 17–27 millimetres in length and those of the Gaboon viper are 45 millimetres long!

In general, the fangs of sea snakes are on the shorter end of the scale for large, dangerous snakes but even so, they are not negligible and they are capable of injecting a lethal dose of venom.

Figure 10.2
Eva Cropp watches as during preparation for a hookah dive, the author finds himself the object of a friendly investigation by an olive sea snake (*Aipysurus laevis*). (Photograph courtesy of Peter Saenger)

AGGRESSIVENESS

Aggressiveness varies greatly among species of sea snakes (Table 10.1). At one extreme are species of the genus *Laticauda* that rarely bite defensively, even under strong provocation. At the other extreme is *Enhydrina schistosa* which can best be described as cantankerous and savage. Most sea snakes will attempt to escape if molested but, like almost any animal, will bite if captured or restrained. There have been sufficient observations on 19 species of hydrophiids and laticaudids to characterise their attitudes toward humans. Of these, six (32 per cent) are innocuous, shy or reluctant to bite, even when provoked. These are *Aipysurus eydouxii, Emydocephalus annulatus, Laticauda colubrina, L. laticaudata, L. schistorhyncha* and *L. semifasciata*. Another nine species (47 per cent) will bite if provoked but seldom or never do so spontaneously. These are *Acalyptophis peronii, Aipysurus duboisii, Aipysurus laevis, Hydrophis coggeri, H. klossi, H. melanosoma, Kerilia jerdoni, Lapemis curtus* and *Pelamis platurus*. Finally there are 4 species (21 per cent) that are more aggressive. *Astrotia stokesii*, although seldom attacking if unprovoked, will bite vigorously and repeatedly when disturbed. The most aggressive species are *Enhydrina schistosa, Hydrophis cyanocinctus* and *H. spiralis*; these snakes are easily angered. In addition to the above species, *Thalassophis anomalus, Hydrophis caerulescens* and possibly *H. ornatus* have been known to bite humans and, although their general temperament has not been reported, they may be aggressive.

The aggressiveness of only one species, *Aipysurus laevis*, has been studied in detail. It is the species most often encountered by divers on reefs and it warrants discussion. There were conflicting reports from divers that ranged from accounts of extreme aggressiveness and unprovoked attacks to belief that this species was docile. The truth lies somewhere between. Under most circumstances this snake either ignores humans in the water or appears curious and investigates them. It often approaches them and protrudes its tongue so as to touch a person as though attempting to pick up an identifying odour. On occasions it follows a diver or wraps itself around an arm or leg (Figure 10.2) with no apparent aggressive intention. However, attacks have occurred.

I set out deliberately to provoke snakes of this species as a means of finding out what induced attacks on humans and to enable me to recommend to divers ways of avoiding unpleasant encounters. Striking a snake with a flipper sometimes discourages further attention and a snake will flee but at other times it induces attack. Attacks provoked in this way are readily distinguishable from curious approaches. They are at high speed and characterised by a 'jerky' head motion. On one occasion an attacking snake repeatedly bit the observer's wet suit. Attacks are persistent and snakes sometimes pursue a retreating diver for up to 100 metres (Figure 10.3), the attack being broken off even then only by capture of the snake or exit of the diver from the water.

Lest this qualitative description of behaviour give a distorted impression of aggressiveness of the olive sea snake, it should be placed in context. Even severe provocation induces attack by only a small proportion of individuals. During early ecological studies that I carried out on this species in collaboration with Peter Saenger, hundreds of snakes were captured, their tails pierced and metal tags affixed, and then the snakes were released (Figure 10.4 and Plate 26). Although such snakes frequently bit the restraining tongs during this process, only 3 per cent attacked once released. Later Glen Burns and I continued marking snakes for several years using gentler methods of catching and handling and there were no further attacks in the water (although three of us sustained one bite each in the laboratory while handling snakes). To date, myself and my collaborators have captured or observed several thousand individuals of this species underwater and have examined other divers' accounts of encounters. We can authenticate only two instances of spontaneous, unprovoked attack. It does seem that attack requires less provocation when snakes are in breeding condition, especially if disturbed during courtship. In conclusion, this species is rarely a threat unless maltreated but, if captured or molested, it may attack. Unprovoked attacks are sufficiently rare to rank less likely than a lightning strike. The key to safe diving with sea snakes is sensible, intelligent behaviour on the part of the intruding diver.

Figure 10.3
An olive sea snake (*Aipysurus laevis*), attacking Peter Saenger. The snake had just been caught and a metal tag affixed to its tail. When released, it launched a persistent attack. (Photograph by the author)

Figure 10.4
A recaptured olive sea snake (*Aipysurus laevis*) showing a numbered fishery tag on the tail. (Photograph by the author)

SYMPTOMS OF SEA SNAKE BITE

There is no pain or swelling at the site of a sea krait or hydrophiid bite other than what one would experience from the mechanical effect of a needle the same size as the fang. Nor is there usually any subsequent necrosis or discolouration of tissue around the puncture (Plate 29). The time until systemic symptoms first appear varies and may depend upon the amount of venom received, the site at which it was injected and the health of the victim. Not all patients experience the same symptoms or in the same sequence.

There are three major categories of symptoms that indicate severe envenomation. The most severe one, rapid collapse and shock, is extremely rare and only occurs if there has been massive envenomation. This response should not be confused with ordinary fainting, which sometimes occurs after a bite and from which the patient soon recovers.

The symptoms of the second category are muscular. Within half an hour of a severe bite the muscles may begin to ache and become stiff, often at sites remote from the bite. Those of the jaws may undergo spasms. After one or two hours, the pain may become moderate to severe when the limbs, neck or trunk are moved, even passively, by an outside agent. The muscles of the eyelids cease to function properly and the eyelids droop uncontrollably. There also may be drowsiness, vomiting and visual disturbances.

The third kind of symptom appears from three to six hours after the bite and results from deterioration of the muscles. When the muscle fibres break down, a muscle pigment, myoglobin, is released and appears in the urine. At high concentrations it stains the urine a mahogany colour, a symptom of serious envenomation. Damaged muscles also release the enzyme creatine kinase into the blood plasma. Chemical tests have been devised that can detect this substance and are used in clinical diagnosis of envenomation.

If medical treatment is not provided when the more severe of the above symptoms occur, the patient is likely to become progressively paralysed to the point of complete immobility and respiratory distress, and in a life-threatening situation. Death from a lethal envenomation usually occurs within 12 to 24 hours but may take up to two days. Patients who recover from serious bites may show permanent muscular wastage and disability, and may suffer permanent kidney damage.

Not all of the symptoms related above for humans apply to laboratory mice. Mice seem to be more susceptible than humans to the neurotoxic components of sea snake venom and die from asphyxiation through malfunction of the nerves to the muscles of the diaphragm that controls breathing. This is reminiscent of the effect of sea snake venom on the snakes' natural prey; recall that fish die from asphyxiation caused by failure of the muscles operating the operculum (see Chapter 9).

Mice do not show overt signs of muscle damage but do develop kidney damage. Shantay Zimmerman injected mice with doses of sea snake (*Aipysurus laevis*) venom so weak that the mice survived the neurotoxic effects. However, over the following month, these mice developed progressive damage to their kidneys. There was inflammation and damage to some of the tubules and blood vessels, followed by the appearance of dark deposits in the glomeruli, dilation of the tubules and finally deterioration and death of tissue, leaving large holes in the kidney (Figure 9.6, page 102). In the later stages some of the mice died.

Humans also suffer kidney damage from sea snake envenomation and in some cases, have died from renal failure. Autopsies of people killed by sea snakes or biopsy samples taken from severely envenomated individuals show structural damage. Unlike mice, there is also considerable muscle damage, sometimes involving death of up to 60 per cent of certain muscle masses. It is the skeletal muscles that are damaged; smooth muscle and heart muscle does not seem to be affected. Humans also may suffer swelling, structural damage and haemorrhage of the liver in response to sea snake bite.

TREATMENT OF SEA SNAKE BITE

There are two kinds of treatment:

1. first aid or the immediate treatment provided by the victim or his or her companions
2. medical treatment, provided by specialists after the patient comes under their care.

These differ and will be treated sequentially.

FIRST AID

Methods of first aid in cases of sea snake bite have undergone considerable improvement as a result of research by Dr Struan Sutherland and his colleagues on laboratory animals, especially monkeys. Procedures previously recommended for snake bite generally, such as application of a tourniquet, or cutting at the site of the bite and sucking it, are now known to be ineffective at best and harmful at worst when applied to bites by sea snakes or terrestrial elapids. None of these techniques should be used for these kinds of snakes.

It is important to keep the victim as still and calm as possible and to prevent the spread of the venom from the site of the bite. If the bite is on a limb, a pressure bandage should be applied as soon as possible. Crepe bandages are best but if not available can be substituted by strips torn from clothing, towelling or bedding. The cloth should be wrapped firmly around the limb at the site of the bite and then outward in both directions from it. As large an area as is practical should be wrapped. For example, if a finger is bitten, the wrapping should include the finger, hand and the arm at least to the elbow. Unlike a tourniquet, such a pressure bandage can be left on for an extended time without damage to the limb; also, it is more effective in keeping the venom localised. Once the bandage is in place, the limb should be restrained in some appropriate way, such as a sling, so that the patient moves it as little as possible. Any muscular action, especially of the affected limb, accelerates distribution of the venom.

The above treatment, if executed immediately, can restrict the venom for a considerable number of hours and under most circumstances provides ample time to get the patient to medical facilities. This knowledge does much to reassure the patient and to restore calm.

The bandage should be left on until the patient is under observation by a medical doctor. Failure of symptoms to appear in a person who has received appropriate first aid does not mean there has been no envenomation. If the venom is effectively isolated near the site of the bite by the bandage, symptoms will be delayed. Premature removal of the bandage may result in serious deterioration of the patient's condition.

First aid to bites of the trunk, neck or head is much less effective as pressure bandages are not easily applied. In such cases, it is especially important to seek immediate medical aid. Fortunately, such bites are not common; ninety-five per cent of snake bites are to the limbs.

MEDICAL TREATMENT

Antivenoms (also called antivenenes or antivenins) are available for the treatment of sea snake bite. Some have been developed especially for particular species of sea snake. If an appropriate one for the specific sea snake involved is not available, antivenom for the tiger snake (an Australian terrestrial elapid, *Notechis scutatus*) is effective if used in large quantities. Even polyvalent Australian antivenom can be used if a more appropriate one is not available. Antivenom for cobras or land kraits do not seem to be very effective against sea snakes.

Antivenoms themselves can be health risks because of the possibility of serum allergy and anaphylactic shock, and in extreme cases can cause death unless dealt with appropriately. Antivenoms should be administered only by a medical doctor unless there is no other option. Indeed in some countries it is illegal for anyone else to do so. Because of the risk in their use, antivenoms should not be used as a matter of course in cases of sea snake bite, even by trained medical practitioners. Rather the patient should be observed and antivenom withheld until the appearance of symptoms of severe envenomation, such as droopy eyelids or myoglobin in the urine. Until then, there is still ample time for effective use of antivenom.

When severe symptoms do develop, it is important that antivenom be administered in order to save life or prevent long-term disability. Antivenoms have been used successfully as long as one or two days after a bite. When antivenoms are used, supplies of adrenaline and antihistamines should be at hand to meet emergencies in the event of serum sickness. Respirators can be used to keep severely envenomated patients alive until other treatments bring about recovery. Dialysis can be used to treat patients suffering from kidney damage and there have been cases of successful treatment by haemodialysis without use of antivenom.

HUMAN FATALITIES FROM SEA SNAKE BITES

At least seven species of sea snakes have been implicated in human fatalities (Table 10.1). *Enhydrina schistosa* is the main killer of humans, being responsible for over half of sea snake bites and for almost 90 per cent of the fatalities resulting from them. *Hydrophis cyanocinctus* is the second most dangerous species and accounts for most of the remaining deaths.

Attempts to catch snakes for scientific or commercial purposes carry the risk of snake bite. In some parts of the world, certain occupations, like fishing, include sea snake bite as a normal occupational hazard and different methods of fishing or snake-catching carry different degrees of risk.

The methods of catching sea snakes vary greatly. Catching by hand, sometimes aided by nooses, dive bags, specially designed snake tongs or merely gloves, is commonly used for obtaining small numbers. Dip-netting at night from the surface using lights that allegedly attract snakes is also employed. Some species are occasionally taken on lines by fishermen. In the Ryukyus, snake fishermen may sit on the edge of an island at night, aided by a hand torch, to catch laticaudids making their forays to and from the sea. In the Philippines, dead fish are laid out as individual baits or placed inside fish traps. Before the practice was outlawed, dynamite was used widely to blast coral reefs and the snakes coming to eat the dead fish often brought a better price (for leather) than did the fish. In some places seining or trawling for fish or prawns nets considerable numbers of sea snakes as a by-catch.

The more direct the contact with the snake, the greater the risk involved. There have been several bites, although not severe ones, from handling sick snakes washed up on beaches. In addition, accidental contact with sea snakes may result in bites. Snakes coming up in trawls, especially trawls of long duration, probably have exhausted their venom through repeated biting of the mesh and other animals during confinement in the net. Trawlermen bitten by such snakes seldom suffer more than brief dizziness or headaches. There have been instances of divers being attacked by sea snakes while making underwater repairs to ships.

The risk may not even be direct. In the Torres Strait a diver suffered the bends as a result of panic upon the approach of a sea snake. He rapidly surfaced without stopping to decompress.

There are ecological and geographic differences in the incidence of sea snake bite. Harold Cogger and I have reviewed the case histories of sea snake bite in Australia in a book edited by P. Gopalakrishnakone called *Sea Snake Toxinology*. Despite the fact that four Australian species of Hydrophiidae (*Enhydrina schistosa*, *Hydrophis ornatus*, *Lapemis curtus* and *Pelamis platurus*) have caused human fatalities elsewhere, there have been no fully substantiated reports of fatality from any species of sea snake within Australia. I have seen newspaper reports of two fatalities presumed to be caused by sea snake bite, one in the Torres Straits and one in Western Australia, but was unable to authenticate either of them. Another reported fatality from *Pelamis platurus* may have resulted from other causes. A child was bitten repeatedly by an *Astrotia stokesii* in Yeppoon and suffered severe symptoms but survived because her mother clamped her hands over the bitten areas and got the child to a nearby hospital immediately where expert medical treatment was administered quickly. Other cases were of lesser consequence, although some involved severe envenomation.

The lack of fatalities in Australia may be related to local fishing methods. Although *Enhydrina schistosa*, which is responsible for many human deaths elsewhere, does occur in Australian waters, few people enter the muddy estuaries constituting its habitat. Hand-seining for fish in such places is rarely practised and muddy areas are not attractive for diving, recreational swimming or water sports. The main contact with sea snakes is by trawling, which does not carry as great a risk (see this page, above). The snakes inhabiting coral reefs, where there is more frequent contact with divers and snorkelers, are less prone to attack humans. In Malaysia it has been estimated that on bathing beaches the risk of dying by drowning is ten-fold greater than suffering a fatal sea snake bite.

In southeastern Asia, bare-footed fishermen using hand-seines in muddy estuaries where sea snakes are abundant run a greater risk. Alistair Reid reviewed the incidence of sea snake bite in Malaysia from

1956 to 1979 and thereafter reported on specific Malaysian localities. About 80 per cent of the then known sea snake bites were inflicted on fishermen, either while handling the contents of their seines (44 per cent) or because of treading upon snakes in the murky water (36 per cent). However, reliable statistics on the incidence of sea snake bite and of the resulting fatalities were difficult to assemble. Few official records are kept in remote fishing villages and many incidents go unreported. There are a number of superstitions surrounding snake bite that inhibit the divulging of information. Consequently available statistics may underestimate incidence of sea snake bite; however, Reid's data for Malaysia suggest values of at least 3.00–3.75 bites per 1000 inhabitants of fishing villages per year. Some of these bites were harmless in that no venom was injected; one estimate was that 68 per cent of sea snake bites were such blanks, with only 22 per cent being truly serious. The incidence of fatalities varied with time and place from 3.2 per cent to nearly 30 per cent of the bites.

In Malaysia people often prefer to rely on ineffective home remedies rather than seek medical attention. Reid reported that in 17 fishing villages 28.5 per cent of the known bites had proved to be fatal but only 12.5 per cent of the victims had gone to a hospital or dispensary. These values may now have changed in response to improved education and greater availability of antivenoms and medical facilities.

In the book *Sea Snake Toxinology* edited by P. Gopalakrishnakone David Warrell reviewed the incidence of sea snake bites in various parts of the world. In Thailand a 1926 report had indicated fatalities from sea snake bite from nearly every fishing village but between 1965 and 1968 the incidence of fatalities was only about 5 per cent. Since then only one death has been reported.

Sea snake bite is frequent in Vietnam, with two to three bites per day having been reported for one beach at the height of the fishing season among fisherman taking the catch out of nets. High incidences of bites have been retained up through recent years in some regions. In the Phat Thiet area the recent incidence of fatalities was 67 per cent (20 deaths from 30 bites in one year). In some areas at least, superstition still prevents effective treatment.

In the Ryukyus, although land snake bites are a serious problem, deaths from sea snakes do not occur. The marine snakes harvested for commercial purposes there (*Laticauda semifasciata*) have docile dispositions.

Many bites by sea snakes occur in India but no systematic study is available to assess the incidence either of bites or fatalities.

In Bangladesh fisherman reported numerous fatalities from sea snake bite but a 1991 survey brought to light only two fatalities in ten years.

Data from Sri Lanka, Burma, Indonesia, the Philippines, Hong Kong, Taiwan and the southwestern Pacific islands are anecdotal and merely indicate that bites have occurred, mostly to fisherman, and that in some of these areas there have been fatalities.

It is clear that in most of the geographic range of sea snakes, fishermen are the most frequent victims, with incidences among other people being quite low. In parts of southeastern Asia, the incidence of fatalities seems to be decreasing, perhaps because of an increasing acceptance of modern medical treatment.

APPENDIX

THE MARINE SNAKES OF THE WORLD AND THEIR DISTRIBUTIONS

FAMILY, GENUS AND SPECIES	DISTRIBUTION RANGE

HYDROPHIIDAE

Acalyptophis
peronii — Coasts of southern New Guinea and northern Australia through the Arafura Sea to the Barrier Reef and New Caledonia

Aipysurus
apraefrontalis — Coast of Western Australia to Ashmore Reef and west into the Timor Sea
duboisii — Waters of northern and western Australia and southern New Guinea, and east to New Caledonia
eydouxii — Coasts of Malaysia, Gulf of Thailand, Vietnam, Indonesia, New Guinea and northern Australia
foliosquama — Ashmore and Hibernia Reefs off the northwestern coast of Australia
fuscus — Reefs between northwestern Australia and Timor
laevis — Waters of the Australian–New Guinean continental shelf, east to New Caledonia
pooleorum — Midwestern coast of northwestern Australia
tenuis — Northwestern coast of Australia and the Arafura Sea

Astrotia
stokesii   Arabian Gulf, Pakistan, India, Sri Lanka and Malaysia east to China and the Australian–New Guinean continental shelf

Disteira
kingii   Seas of northern Australia
major   Coasts of southen New Guinea, Arafura Sea and coastal waters from northwestern Australia to eastern Queensland
nigrocincta   Coasts of India, Sri Lanka and Burma
walli   Malayan archipelago

Emydocephalus
annulatus   Waters of tropical Australia from the Timor Sea to the southwestern Pacific Ocean
ijimae   Coasts of China, Taiwan and Japan

Enhydrina
schistosa   Arabian Gulf to Pakistan, India and Sri Lanka, east to Australia and New Guinea and north to Vietnam

Ephalophis
greyi   Waters of northwestern Australia

Hydrelaps
darwiniensis   Shallow coastal waters of northern Australia and southern New Guinea

Hydrophis
(excluding *H. semperi,* known only from a freshwater lake)
atriceps   Australian and New Guinean waters west into Indonesia
belcheri   Indo-Malayan waters east to New Guinea
bituberculatus   Coasts of Sri Lanka
brookii   Indonesia, coasts of Malaysia and Gulf of Thailand
caerulescens   Coasts of Pakistan, India, Sri Lanka, east to northern Australia and the Gulf of Thailand
cantoris   Coasts of Pakistan, India, Sri Lanka, Burma and the western Malay Peninsula
coggeri   The Coral Sea east to Fiji
cyanocinctus   Arabian Gulf east to Indonesia, the Philippine Islands, China and Japan
czeblukovi   Australia
elegans   Waters of northern Australia and southern New Guinea
fasciatus   Coasts of Pakistan, India and Sri Lanka, east to Indonesia and the Philippine Islands
geometricus   Seas off northwestern Australia
gracilis   Arabian and Oman Gulfs, east to Indonesia, the Gulf of Papua and China
inornatus   Coasts of the Philippines, south to the Arafura Sea and the Australian–New Guinean continental shelf
klossi   Gulf of Thailand south to Indonesia
lapemoides   Arabian Gulf east to India and Sri Lanka

mamillaris	Coasts of Pakistan, India and Sri Lanka
mcdowelli	Australian–New Guinean continental shelf
melanocephalus	Coasts of China, Taiwan and Japan
melanosoma	Eastern coast of the Malay Peninsula through Indonesia to north western Australia and southern New Guinea
obscurus	Coasts of eastern India and the waters of Sri Lanka and Burma
ocellatus	Coasts of southern New Guinea and northern Australia
ornatus	Arabian Gulf, east to Indonesia, China and Taiwan
pacificus	Eastern Arafura Sea, east through the Australian–New Guinean continental shelf
parviceps	Cochin, China
spiralis	Arabian Gulf, east to Indonesia and the Philippines
stricticollis	Coasts of eastern India, Sri Lanka and Burma
torquatus	Straits of Malacca, Gulf of Thailand and eastern coast of the Malay Peninsula to Borneo (3 subspecies)
vorisi	Australia and New Guinea

Kerilia
jerdoni	Bay of Bengal east through the Straits of Malacca to the Gulf of Thailand and Indonesia (2 subspecies)

Kolpophis
annandalei	Gulf of Thailand south to Indonesia

Lapemis
curtus	Arabian Gulf east through the Bay of Bengal and the Gulf of Thailand to the Australian–New Guinean continental shelf and the waters of the Philippine Islands

Parahydrophis
mertoni	Arafura Sea

Pelamis
platurus	Coasts of eastern Africa, north to the Arabian Gulf, then east along the Asian coast of the Indian Ocean to the Pacific Ocean, northward to Japan and eastward to the western coasts of the Americas

Thalassophina
viperina	Arabian Gulf to Pakistan, around India to Indonesia and southern China

Thalassophis
anomalus	Gulf of Thailand south to Indonesia

LATICAUDIDAE
(excluding *L. crockeri*, a freshwater species)

Laticauda
colubrina	Coasts of Sri Lanka and eastern India, east through Malaysia, Indonesia, New Guinea and the Philippine Islands to the islands of the southwestern Pacific Ocean and northward to China, Taiwan and Japan; at least as strays to Australia and New Zealand

laticaudata	Coasts of Sri Lanka and eastern India, east to Malaysia, Indonesia, New Guinea and the islands of the southwestern Pacific Ocean, northward to China, Taiwan and Japan
schistorhyncha	Niue
semifasciata	Philippine Islands, Taiwan, China and Japan

COLUBRIDAE
(excluding the terrestrial and strictly freshwater species)
HOMALOPSINAE

Bitia
hydroides	Coastal areas of Burma, Thailand and Malaysia

Cantoria
annulata	Coasts of New Guinea
violacea	Coasts of Burma and Malaysia

Cerberus
rynchops	Southeastern Asia, the East Indian archipelago and northern Australia

Enhydris
bennetti	China
chinensis	China

Fordonia
leucobalia	Southeastern Asia, the East Indian archipelago and northern Australia

Gerarda
provostiana	India to Thailand

Myron
richardsonii	New Guinea and Australia

NATRICINAE

Nerodia
fasciata	Three subspecies from salty habitats collectively occur in Cuba and along the coasts of the Gulf of Mexico and the southern Atlantic seaboard of the United States
sipedon	A subspecies (*williamengelsi*) from a salty habitat occurs on the coast of North Carolina, USA
valida	Pacific coast of Mexico

ACROCHORDIDAE
(excluding two strictly freshwater species)

Acrochordus
granulatus	Coastal areas from India and Sri Lanka to Indonesia, Malaysia, the Indo-Chinese Peninsula, northern Australia, the Philippine Islands, New Guinea and the Solomon Islands

FURTHER READING

The literature on sea snakes is scattered widely. A recent, comprehensive bibliography on the Hydrophiidae and Laticaudidae, compiled by Culotta and Pickwell lists about 2500 articles. This valuable work is arranged and indexed by topic. Persons wishing to delve more deeply into the biology of sea snakes would be rewarded by consulting this reference:

Culotta, WA and Pickwell, GV (1993) *The Venomous Sea Snakes: a Comprehensive Bibliography,* Krieger Publishing Company, Malabar, Florida.

GENERAL REFERENCES

Dunson, WA (1975) *Biology of Sea Snakes*, University Park Press, Baltimore.

Greer, E (1997) *The Biology and Evolution of Australian Snakes*, Surrey Beatty & Sons Pty. Ltd., Chipping Norton.

Heuvelmans, B (1968) *In the Wake of Sea Serpents*, Hill and Wang, New York.

CHAPTER 1: WHAT ARE SEA SNAKES?

Burger, WL and Natsuno, T (1974) A new genus for the Arafura smooth seasnake and redefinitions of other seasnake genera, *The Snake* 6: 61–75.

Cadle, JE and Gorman, GC (1981) Albumin immunological evidence and the relationships of sea snakes, *Journal of Herpetology* 15: 329–334.

Dunson, WA and Ehlert, GW (1971) Effects of temperature, salinity, and surface water flow on distribution of the sea snake, *Pelamis. Limnology and Oceanography* 16: 845–853.

Golay, P, Smith, HM, Broadley, DG, Dixon, JR, McCarthy, C, Rage, J-C, Schatti, B and Toriba, M (1993) *Endoglyphs and other Major Venomous Snakes of the World. A Checklist*, Azemiops SA, Herpetological Data Center, Geneva.

Gyi, KK (1970) A revision of colubrid snakes of the subfamily Homalopsinae, *Publications of the University of Kansas Museum of Natural History* 20: 47–223.

McDowell, SD (1969) Notes on the Australian sea-snake *Ephalophis greyi* M. Smith (Serpentes: Elapidae: Hydrophiinae) and the origin and classification of sea-snakes, *Zoological Journal of the Linnean Society* 48: 333–349.

Smith, M (1926) *Monograph of the Sea-Snakes (Hydrophiidae)*, British Museum (Natural History), London.

Voris, HK (1977) A phylogeny of the sea snakes (Hydrophiidae), *Fieldiana (Zoology)* 70: 79–169.

Wright, AH and Wright, AA (1957) *Handbook of Snakes of the United States and Canada*, Comstock Publishing Associates, Ithaca.

CHAPTER 2: DISTRIBUTION AND BIODIVERSITY

Campden-Main, SM (1970) *A Field Guide to the Snakes of South Vietnam*, Smithsonian Institution, Washington DC.

Cogger, HG (1992) *Reptiles & Amphibians of Australia*, Reed Books, Chatswood, Australia.

Department of the Navy (1962) *Poisonous Snakes of the World, a Manual for Use by U.S. Amphibious Forces*, US Government Printing Office, Washington DC.

de Silva, A (1994) An account of the sea snakes (Serpentes: Hydrophiidae) of Sri Lanka, in *Sea Snake Toxinology* (ed Gopalakrishnakone, P), Singapore University Press, Singapore.

Dunson, WA and Minton, SA (1978) Diversity, distribution and ecology of Philippine marine snakes (Reptilia, Serpentes), *Journal of Herpetology* 12: 281–286.

Guinea, ML Sea snakes of Fiji and Niue (1994), in *Sea Snake Toxinology* (ed Gopalakrishnakone, P), Singapore University Press: Singapore.

Heatwole, H. and Cogger, H. (1994) Sea snakes of Australia, in *Sea Snake Toxinology* (ed Gopalakrishnakone, P), Singapore University Press, Singapore.

Hu, B, Huang, M, Xie, Z, Zhao, E, Jiang, Y, Huang, C and Ma, J (1980) *The Atlas of Snakes in China* [in Chinese], Shanghai Science and Technology Publishing Company, Shanghai.

Mao, S-H and Chen, B-Y (1980) *Sea Snakes of Taiwan*, The National Science Council, Taipei.

McCoy, M (1980) Reptiles of the Solomon Islands, *Wau Ecology Institute Handbook* No. 7: 1–80.

Minton, SA Jr. (1966) A contribution to the herpetology of West Pakistan, *Bulletin of the American Museum of Natural History* 134: 27–184.

Minton, SA Jr. and Dunson, W (1985) Sea snakes collected at Chesterfield Reefs, Coral Sea. *Atoll Research Bulletin* No. 292: 101–108.

Murthy, TSN (1986) *The Snake Book of India*, International Book Distributors, Dehra Dun, India.

O'Shea, M (1996) *A Guide to the Snakes of Papua New Guinea*, Independent Publishing, Port Moresby.

Taylor, EH (1922) *The Snakes of the Philippine Islands*, Department of Agriculture and Natural Resources, Manila.

Toriba, M (1994) Sea snakes of Japan, in *Sea Snake Toxinology* (ed Gopalakrishnakone, P), Singapore University Press, Singapore.

Zhao, E-M and Adler, K (1993) Herpetology of China, Society for the Study of Amphibians and Reptiles, *Contributions to Herpetology* 10: 1–522.

Zimmerman, KD, Heatwole, H and Menez, A (1994) Sea snakes in the Coral Sea: an expedition for the collection of animals and venom, *Herpetofauna* 24: 25–29.

CHAPTER 3: NATURAL HISTORY

Burns, GW (1984) Aspects of Population Movements and Reproductive Biology of *Aipysurus laevis*, the Olive Sea Snake, PhD dissertation, University of New England, Armidale, NSW.

Burns, G and Heatwole, H (1998) Home range and habitat use of the Olive Sea Snake, *Aipysurus laevis*, on the Great Barrier Reef, Australia, *Journal of Herpetology* 32: 350–358.

Cogger, HG, Heatwole, H, Ishikawa, Y, McCoy, M, Tamiya, N and Teruuchi, T (1987) The status and natural history of the Rennell

Island sea krait, *Laticauda crockeri* (Serpentes: Laticaudidae), *Journal of Herpetology* 21: 255–266.

Gorman, GC, Licht, P and McColllum, F (1981) Annual reproductive patterns in three species of marine snakes from the central Philippines, *Journal of Herpetology* 15: 335-354.

Graham, JB, Rubinoff, I and Hecht, MK (1971) Temperature physiology of the sea snake *Pelamis platurus*: an index of its colonization potential in the Atlantic Ocean, *Proceedings of the National Academy of Science*, USA 68: 1360–1363.

Heatwole, H and Cogger, HG (1993) Family Hydrophiidae, in *Fauna of Australia*, volume 2A *Amphibia & Reptilia* (eds Glasby, CJ, Ross, GJB and Beesley, PL) Australian Government Publishing Service, Canberra.

Heatwole, H and Guinea, ML (1993) Family Laticaudidae, in *Fauna of Australia*, volume 2A *Amphibia & Reptilia* (eds Glasby, CJ, Ross, GJB and Beesley, PL) Australian Government Publishing Service, Canberra.

Voris, HK and Jayne, BC (1979) Growth, reproduction and population structure of a marine snake, *Enhydrina schistosa* (Hydrophiidae), *Copeia* 1979: 307–318.

Zimmerman, K and Heatwole, H (1990) Cutaneous photoreception: a new sensory mechanism for reptiles, *Copeia* 1990: 860–862.

CHAPTER 4: FOOD AND FEEDING

Guinea, ML (1996) Functions of the cephalic scales of the sea snake *Emydocephalus anulatus*. *Journal of Herpetology* 30: 126–128.

Heatwole, H (1977) Adaptations of sea snakes, pp. 193–204 in *Australian Animals and their Environments* (eds Messel, H and Butler, ST), Shakespeare Head Press, Sydney.

Jayne, BC, Ward, TJ and Voris, HK (1995) Morphology, reproduction, and diet of the marine homalopsine snake *Bitia hydroides* in peninsular Malaysia, *Copeia* 1995: 800–808.

Jayne, BC, Voris, HK and Heang, KB (1988) Diet, feeding behavior, growth, and numbers of a population of *Cerberus rynchops* (Serpentes: Homalopsinae) in Malaysia, *Fieldiana* (*Zoology*) *New Series* No. 30: 1–15.

McCosker, JE (1975) Feeding behavior of Indo-Australian Hydrophiidae, pp. 217–232 in *The Biology of Sea Snakes* (ed Dunson, WA), University Park Press, Baltimore.

Voris, HK and Voris, HH (1983) Feeding strategies in marine snakes: an analysis of evolutionary, morphological, behavioral and ecological relationships, *American Zoologist* 23: 411–425.

Voris, HK, Voris, HH and Liat, LB (1978) The food and feeding behavior of a marine snake, *Enhydrina schistosa*, (Hydrophiidae), *Copeia* 1978: 134–146.

CHAPTER 5: ENEMIES

Heatwole, H (1975) Predation on sea snakes, pp. 233–249 in *The Biology of Sea Snakes* (ed Dunson, WA). University Park Press, Baltimore.

Heatwole, H, Minton, SA Jr., Taylor, R and Taylor, V (1978) Underwater observations on sea snake behaviour, *Records of the Australian Museum* 31: 737–761.

Pickwell, GV (1971) Knotting and coiling behavior in the pelagic sea snake *Pelamis platurus* L, *Copeia* 1971: 348–350.

Rubinoff, I and Kropach, C (1970) Differential reactions of Atlantic and Pacific predators to sea snakes, *Nature* 226: 1288–1290.

Voris, HK and Jeffries, WB (1995) Predation on marine snakes: a case for decapods supported by new observations from Thailand, *Journal of Tropical Ecology* 11: 569–576.

Weldon, PJ (1988) Feeding responses of Pacific snappers (genus *Lutjanus*) to the yellow-bellied sea snake (*Pelamis platurus*), *Zoological Science* 5: 443–448.

CHAPTER 6: POPULATION AND COMMUNITY ECOLOGY

Burns, GW (1984) Aspects of Population Movements and Reproductive Biology of *Aipysurus laevis*, the Olive Sea Snake, PhD dissertation, University of New England, Armidale, NSW.

Hin, HK, Steubing, RB and Voris, HK (1991) Population structure and reproduction in the marine snake, *Lapemis hardwickii* Gray, from the west coast of Sabah, *Sarawak Museum Journal* 42: 463–475.

Jayne, BC, Voris, HK and Heang, KB (1988) Diet, feeding, behavior, growth, and numbers of a population of *Cerberus rynchops* (Serpentes: Homalopsinae) in Malaysia, *Fieldiana, Zoology, New Series* No. 50: 1–15.

Lading, EA, Stuebing, RB and Voris, HK (1991) A population size estimate of the yellow-lipped sea krait, *Laticauda colubrina*, on Kalampunian Damit Island, Sabah, Malaysia. *Copeia* 1991: 1139–1142.

Lemen, CA and Voris, HK (1981) A comparison of reproductive strategies among marine snakes, *Journal of Animal Ecology* 50: 89–101.

Saint Girons, H (1990) Notes on ecology and population structure of the Laticaudinae (Serpentes, Hydrophidae) in New Caledonia, *Bulletin of the Chicago Herpetological Society* 25: 197–209.

Steubing, R and Voris, HK (1990) Relative abundance of marine snakes on the west coast of Sabah, Malaysia, *Journal of Herpetology* 24: 201–202.

Voris, HK (1985) Population size estimates for a marine snake (*Enhydrina schistosa*) in Malaysia, *Copeia* 1985: 955–961.

Voris, HK and Voris, HH (1983) Feeding strategies in marine snakes, an analysis of evolutionary, morphological behavioral and ecological relationships, *American Zoologist* 23: 411–425.

Wassenberg, TJ, Salini, JP, Heatwole, H and Kerr, JD (1994) Incidental capture of sea-snakes (Hydrophiidae) by prawn trawlers in the Gulf of Carpentaria, Australia, *Australian Journal of Marine and Freshwater Research* 48: 429–443.

CHAPTER 7: ADAPTATIONS TO LIFE IN SALT WATER

Dunson, WA (1968) Salt gland secretion in the pelagic sea snake *Pelamis. American Journal of Physiology* 215: 1512–1517.

Dunson, WA (1978) Role of the skin in sodium and water exchange of aquatic snakes placed in seawater, *American Journal of Physiology* 235: R151–R159.

Dunson, WA (1979) Control mechanisms in reptiles, in *Mechanisms of Osmoregulation* (ed Gilles, R) John Wiley and Sons, New York.

Dunson, WA (1980) The relation of sodium and water balance to survival in sea water of estuarine and freshwater races of the snakes *Nerodia fasciata, N. sipedon* and *N. valida, Copeia* 1980: 268-280.

Dunson, WA and Dunson, MK (1973) Convergent evolution of sublingual salt glands in the marine file snake and the true sea snakes, *Journal of Comparative Physiology* 86: 193–208.

Dunson, WA and Dunson, MK (1974) Interspecific differences in fluid concentration and secretion rate of sea snake salt glands, *American Journal of Physiology* 227: 430–438.

Dunson, WA and Robinson, GD (1976) Sea snake skin: permeable to water but not to sodium, *Journal of Comparative Physiology* 108: 303–311.

Dunson, WA and Stokes, GD (1983) Asymmetrical diffusion of sodium and water through the skin of sea snakes, *Physiological Zoology* 56: 106–111.

Dunson, WA and Taub, AM (1967) Extrarenal salt excretion in sea snakes (*Laticauda*), *American Journal of Physiology* 213: 975–982.

Guinea, M (1991) Rainwater drinking by the sea krait *Laticauda colubrina*, *Herpetofauna* 21: 13–14.

Heatwole, H (1977) Adaptations of sea snakes, in *Australian Animals and their Environments*, (ed Messel, H and Butler, ST), Shakespeare Head Press, Sydney.

Heatwole, H (1978) Adaptations of marine snakes, *American Scientist* 66: 594–604.

Heatwole, H and Taylor, J (1987) *Ecology of Reptiles*, Surrey Beatty and Sons Pty. Ltd.: Chipping Norton, NSW.

Zug, DA and Dunson, WA (1979) Salinity preferences in fresh water and estuarine snakes (*Nerodia sipedon* and *N. fasciata*), *Florida Scientist* 42: 1–8.

CHAPTER 8: DIVING ADAPTATIONS

Graham, JB (1974) Body temperatures of the sea snake *Pelamis platurus*, *Copeia* 1974: 531-533.

Graham, J.B (1974) Aquatic respiration in the sea snake *Pelamis platurus*, *Respiration Physiology* 21: 1–7.

Graham, JB, Gee, JH and Robison, FS (1975) Hydrostatic and gas exchange functions of the lung of the sea snake *Pelamis platurus*, *Comparative Biochemistry and Physiology* 50A: 477–482.

Heatwole, H (1975) Voluntary submergence times of marine snakes, *Marine Biology* 32: 205–213.

Heatwole, H (1977) Sea snakes, a contrast to other vertebrate divers, *South Pacific Underwater Medicine Society Journal*, July–December 1977: 35–38.

Heatwole, H (1977) Adaptations of sea snakes, in *Australian Animals and their Environments*, (ed Messel, H and Butler, ST), Shakespeare Head Press, Sydney.

Heatwole, H (1977) Heart rate during breathing and apnea in marine snakes (Reptilia, Serpentes), *Journal of Herpetology* 11: 67–76

Heatwole, H (1978) Adaptations of marine snakes, *American Scientist* 66: 594–604.

Heatwole, H (1981) Role of the saccular lung in the diving of the sea krait *Laticauda colubrina* (Serpentes: Laticaudidae), *Australian Journal of Herpetology* 1: 11–16.

Heatwole, H (1981) Temperature relations of some sea snakes, *The Snake* 13: 53–57.

Heatwole, H and Dunson, WA (1987) Hematological parameters of some marine snakes, *Journal of Experimental Marine Biology and Ecology* 113: 289–300.

Heatwole, H and Seymour, R (1976) Respiration of marine snakes, in

Respiration of Amphibious Vertebrates (ed Hughes, GM) Academic Press, New York.

Heatwole, H and Seymour, R (1978) Cutaneous oxygen uptake in three groups of aquatic snakes, *Australian Journal of Zoology* 26: 481–486.

Heatwole, H, Seymour, R and Webster, MED (1979) Heart rates of sea snakes diving in the sea, *Comparative Biochemistry and Physiology* 62A: 453–456.

Lillywhite, HB, Smits, AW and Feder, ME (1988) Body fluid volumes in the aquatic snake, *Acrochordus granulatus*, *Journal of Herpetology* 22: 434–438.

Pough, FH and Lillywhite, HB (1984) Blood volume and blood oxygen capacity of sea snakes, *Physiological Zoology* 57: 32–39.

Seymour, RS (1976) Blood respiratory properties in a sea snake and a land snake, *Australian Journal of Zoology* 23: 313–320.

Seymour, RS (1982) Physiological adaptations to aquatic life, in *Biology of the Reptilia*, volume 13 *Physiology D, Physiological Ecology* (eds Gans, C and Pough, FH) Academic Press: New York.

Webb, G., Heatwole, H and de Bavay, J (1971) Comparative cardiac anatomy of the Reptilia, I. *Journal of Morphology* 134: 335–350.

CHAPTER 9: VENOM

Guinea, ML, Tamiya, N and Cogger, HG (1983) The neurotoxins of the sea snake *Laticauda schistorhynchus*, *Biochemical Journal* 213: 39–41.

Heatwole, H and Poran, NS (1995) Resistances of sympatric and allopatric eels to sea snake venoms, *Copeia* 1995: 136–147.

Heatwole, H and Powell, J (1998) Resistance of eels (*Gymnothorax*) to the venom of sea kraits (*Laticauda colubrina*): a test of coevolution, *Toxicon* 36: 619–625.

Limpus, CJ (1978) The venom apparatus and venom yields of subtropical Queensland Hydrophiidae, *Toxicon Supplement* 1: 39–70.

Tamiya, N, Sato, A, Kim, HS, Teruuchi, T, Takasaki, C, Ishikawa, Y, Guinea, ML, McCoy, M, Heatwole, H and Cogger, HG (1983) Neurotoxins of sea snakes genus *Laticauda*, *Toxicon*, Supplement 3: 445–447.

Zimmerman, KD and Heatwole, H (1992) Ventilation rates in three prey fish species treated with venom of the olive sea snake, *Aipysurus laevis*, *Comparative Biochemistry and Physiology* 102C: 421–425.

Zimmerman, KD, Gates, GR and Heatwole, H (1990) Effects of venom of the olive sea snake, *Aipysurus laevis*, on the behaviour and ventilation of three species of fish, *Toxicon* 28: 1468–1478.

Zimmerman, KD, Heatwole, H and Davies, HI (1992) Survival times and resistance to sea snake (*Aipysurus laevis*) venom by five species of prey fish, *Toxicon* 30: 259–264.

Zimmerman, KD, Walters, DJ, Hawkins, CJ and Heatwole, H (1993) Effects of fractions isolated from venom of the Olive Sea Snake *Aipysurus laevis* on the behavior and ventilation of a prey species of fish, *Journal of Natural Toxins* 2:175–186.

CHAPTER 10: SEA SNAKES AND HUMANS

Gopalakrishnakone, P (1994) *Sea Snake Toxinology*, Singapore University Press, Singapore.

Heatwole, H (1975) Attacks by sea snakes on divers, pp. 503-516 in *The Biology of Sea Snakes* (ed Dunson, WA), University Park Press, Baltimore.

Heatwole, H (1978) Sea snake attack: Myth or menace? *Skindiving in Australia and New Zealand* 8: 40–45.

Heatwole, H (1997) Marine snakes: are they a sustainable resource? *Wildlife Society Bulletin* 25: 766–772.

Limpus, CJ (1978) Toxicology of the venom of subtropical Queensland Hydrophiidae, *Toxicon Supplement* 1: 341–363.

Sutherland, SK (1983) *Australian Animal Toxins*, Oxford University Press, Melbourne.

Wassenberg, TJ, Salini, JP, Heatwole, H and Kerr, JD (1994) Incidental capture of sea-snakes (Hydrophiidae) by prawn trawlers in the Gulf of Carpentaria, Australia, *Australian Journal of Marine and Freshwater Research* 48: 429–443.

Zimmerman, KD (1988) The question of sea snake aggression. *Herpetofauna* 18: 11–12.

Zimmerman, SE and Heatwole, H (1987) Olive sea snake venom, in *Toxic Plants & Animals, a Guide for Australia,* (ed Covacevich, J, Davie, P and Pearn, J), Queensland Museum, South Brisbane.

Zimmerman, SE, Heatwole, H, Andreopoulos, PC and Yong, LCJ (1992) Proliferative glomerulonephritis in mice induced by sea snake (*Aipysurus laevis*) venom, *Experimental and Toxicologic Pathology* 44: 294–300.

INDEX

Bold page numbers indicate an illustration or diagram; plates refer to the coloured plates. Place names in Appendix 1 and in the captions to the plates are not included in the index, although the species names are.